Detroit Studies in
Music Bibliography

General Editor
Bruno Nettl
University of Illinois at Urbana-Champaign

A
SELECTED
DISCOGRAPHY
OF
SOLO SONG
*
Supplement
*
1971-1974
*
DOROTHY STAHL
*

Detroit Studies in
Music Bibliography 34
*

Information Coordinators, Inc.
Detroit
1976

Book design and illustration
by Vincent Kibildis

Published by
Information Coordinators, Inc.
1435-37 Randolph Street
Detroit, Michigan 48226

CONTENTS

INTRODUCTION

THIS EDITION OF *A Selected Discography of Solo Song* includes the recordings which have been released since 1971.

In the first section, the songs are arranged alphabetically by composer and under composer by title. Cycles are listed under the name of the cycle; when the songs are recorded separately, they are also entered under the title of the song with a reference to the complete cycle. Under the song title is the name of the artist, the title of the recording and the record number. Since many of the recordings consist of miscellaneous programs that include songs by various composers, each song is listed under the name of the composer.

The second section is a list of the releases indexed in the discography and includes the complete contents, the names of the artists in full and the record number. The first of this section's two parts consists of releases of the works of one composer in alphabetical order; the second, releases of works of two or more composers arranged alphabetically by manufacturer, then, numerically by serial number. The contents of the records in each entry are alphabetical by title in the case of works of one composer. Anthologies are arranged alphabetically by composers and under composer by song title. Excerpts are followed by the title of the complete work in parentheses. In some cases, the recordings include compositions that are not within the scope of this index; these are not included in the main discography. This list may be used as a cross-reference with the discography where each title is listed under the name of the composer and which may include several recordings of the same work.

The third section is an index of song titles and first lines in one alphabetical listing. Articles are disregarded in the alphabetical arrangement.

Although there may be some recordings available which are not listed here, it is the intention of this discography to make accessible to teachers and students vocal works on recordings that can be easily procured.

D. S.

Smith College
Northampton, Massachusetts

Label	Abbreviation
ABC	
Angel	Ang
Argo	
BASF	
Bruno Walter Society	BWS
Cambridge	Cam
Cantilena	Cant
Columbia	Col
Coronet	Cor
Composers Recordings, Inc.	CRI
Desto	
DIS	
Duke	
Deutsche Grammophon	DG
DG Archive	
EDUCO	
EMI - Electrola	
Hungaroton	Hung
Klavier	Klav
London	Lon
Melodiya/Angel	Mel/Ang
Musical Heritage Society	MHS
Nonesuch	None
Odeon	
Odyssey	Ody
Oiseau-Lyre	Oiseau
Orion	
Philips	Phi
Pleiades	
Poseidon Society	Pos
RCA	
Richmond	Rich
Rococo	Roc
Seraphim	Sera
Supraphon	Supra
Telefunken	Tel
Turnabout	Turn
Valois	Val

DISCOGRAPHY OF SOLO SONG

ABT, FRANZ (1819-1885)
1   Der Kukuck
     Songs My Mother Taught Me. Joan Sutherland. Col 26378

ADAM, CHARLES (1803-1856)
2   Variations on a theme of Mozart
     Concert. Beverly Sills. ABC ATS 20011

ADAMS, STEPHEN (1844-1913)
3   Nirvana
     Ballads and Songs of Love and Sentiment. Stuart Burrows. Oiseau SOL 324

ALWYN, WILLIAM (1905-
4   Mirages (Undine / Aquarium / Honeysuckle / Metronome / Paradise / Portrait in a mirror)
     William Alwyn. Benjamin Luxon. MHS 1742

ARNE, THOMAS (1710-1778)
5   Bacchus and Ariadne
6   Fair Caelia love pretended
     Robert Tear sings Handel, Arne, Boyce, Hook. Argo ZRG 661
7   The soldier tir'd (Artaxerxes)
     Concert. Beverly Sills. ABC ATS 20011

ARNIM, BETTINA VON (1785-1859)
8   O schaudre nicht
     Frühe Goethe-Lieder. Dietrich Fischer-Dieskau. DG Archive 2533149

ATTAINGNANT, PIERRE (?-1552)
9   Au joly bois
     Album of Ayres. Donna Curry. KLAV KS 513

BACH, CARL PHILIPP EMANUEL (1714-1788)
10   Abendlied (Wq 194)
11   Bitten (Wq 194)
12   Demut (Wq 194)
13   Der Frühling (Wq 197)
14   Die Güte Gottes (Wq 194)
15   Jesus in Gethsemane (Wq 198)
16   Morgengesang (Wq 194)

BACH, CARL PHILIPP EMANUEL— *Continued*
17 Passionslied (Wq 194)
18 Prüfung am Abend (Wq 194)
19 19 Psalm (Wq 196)
20 130 Psalm (Wq 196)
21 148 Psalm (Wq 196)
22 Der Tag des Weltgerichts (Wq 197)
23 Trost der Erlösung (Wq 194)
24 Über die Finsternis kurz vor dem Tode Jesu (Wq 197)
25 Weihnachtslied (Wq 198)
26 Wider den Übermut (Wq 194)
 Odes, Psalms and Lieder. Dietrich Fischer-Dieskau. DG Archive 2533058

BACH, JOHANN SEBASTIAN (1685-1750)
27 Ächzen und erbärmlich Weinen (Cantata No. 13)
28 Lass', o Welt (Cantata No. 123)
 Baroque—Sacred and Profane. Dietrich Fischer-Dieskau. Ang S-36904

BARBER, SAMUEL (1910-
29 The daisies
30 I hear an army
31 Monks and raisins
32 Nocturne
33 Rain has fallen
34 Sleep now
35 Sure on this shining night
36 With rue my heart is laden
 Favorite American Concert Songs. Dale Moore. Cam CRS 2715

BARTOK, BELA (1881-1945)
37 Five songs, Op. 15 (Hungarian) (My love / Summer / Night of desire / In vivid dreams / In the valley)
38 Five songs, Op. 16 (Hungarian) (Autumn tears / Autumn echoes / Lost content / Alone with the sea / I cannot come to you)
39 Five village scenes (Hungarian) (Haymaking / At the bride's / Wedding / Lullaby / Lads' dance)
 Bartók. Julia Hamari. DG 2530405

BEETHOVEN, LUDWIG VAN (1770-1827)
40 An die ferne Geliebte (Auf dem Hügel sitz' ich / Wo die Berge so blau / Leichte Segler in den Höhen / Diese Wolken in den Höhen / Es kehret der Maien / Nimm sie hin denn)
 Recital. John Shirley-Quirk. Argo ZRG 664
41 An die Hoffnung, Op. 94
 Jennie Tourel at Alice Tully Hall. Desto DC 7118-9
42 Bitten
43 Busslied
 Recital. John Shirley-Quirk. Argo ZRG 664
44 Come fill, fill my good fellow (Scottish song)
 Folk Song Arrangements. Dietrich Fischer-Dieskau. DG 2530262
45 Die Ehre Gottes aus der Natur
46 Gottes Macht und Vorsehung
47 Die Liebe des Nächsten
 Recital. John Shirley-Quirk. Argo ZRG 664
48 Mit Mädeln sich vertragen
 Frühe Goethe-Lieder. Dietrich Fischer-Dieskau. DG Archive 2533149

49 Oh, had my fate been join'd at parting
50 Oh sweet were the hours (Scottish songs)
51 Pulse of an Irishman (Irish song)
52 Put round the bright wine (Irish song)
   Folk Song Arrangements. Dietrich Fischer-Dieskau. DG 2530262
53 Vom Tode
   Recital. John Shirley-Quirk. Argo ZRG 664
54 Zärtliche Liebe
   Jennie Tourel at Alice Tully Hall. Desto DC 7118-9

BELLINI, VINCENZO (1801-1835)
55 L'abandono
   Romantic Songs. Lydia Marimpietri. Lon STS 15164
56 L'allegro marinaro
   Italian Chamber Music. Dicran Jamgochian. Cor 2818
57 Almen se non poss'io
   Romantic Songs. Lydia Marimpietri. Lon STS 15164
58 Bella Nice
   Romantic Songs. Ugo Benelli. Lon STS 15164
59 Il fervido Desiderio
   Romantic Songs. Lydia Marimpietri. Lon STS 15164
60 Malinconia, ninfa gentile
   Romantic Songs. Ugo Benelli. Lon STS 15164
   Tebaldi in Concert. Renata Tebaldi. Lon 26303
61 Per pietà, bell'idol mio
   Romantic Songs. Ugo Benelli. Lon STS 15164
62 Quando incise su quel marmo
63 Vaga luna che inargenti
   Italian Chamber Music. Dicran Jamgochian. Cor 2818

BERG, ALBAN (1885-1935)
64 Nun ich der Riesen stärksten überwand
65 Schlafen, schlafen
66 Schlafend trägt man mich
   Songs of the New Vienna School. Dietrich Fischer-Dieskau. DG 2530107
67 Seven early songs (Nacht / Schilflied / Die Nachtigall / Traumgekrönt /
   Im Zimmer / Liebesode / Sommertage)
   Berg. Heather Harper. Col M-32162
68 Warme die Lüfte
   Songs of the New Vienna School. Dietrich Fischer-Dieskau. DG 2530107

BERLIOZ, HECTOR (1803-1869)
69 L'absence
   Jennie Tourel at Alice Tully Hall. Desto DC 7118-9

BISHOP, HENRY ROWLEY (1786-1855)
70 Lo, here the gentle lark
   Concert. Beverly Sills. ABC ATS 20011

BIZET, GEORGES (1838-1875)
71 Absence
   French and Spanish Songs. Marilyn Horne. Lon OS 26301
72 Adieux de l'hôtesse arabe
   French and Spanish Songs. Marilyn Horne. Lon OS 26301
   A Tribute to Jennie Tourel. 2-Ody Y2 32880
73 Chanson d'Avril
74 Vieille chanson
   French and Spanish Songs. Marilyn Horne. Lon OS 26301

BÖHM, KARL (1894-
75   Still as the night
      Ballads and Songs of Love and Sentiment. Stuart Burrows. Oiseau SOL 324

BOND, CARRIE JACOBS (1862-1946)
76   A perfect day
      Ballads and Songs of Love and Sentiment. Stuart Burrows. Oiseau SOL 324

BORODIN, ALEXANDER (1833-1887)
77   For the shores of thy fair native land (Russian)
      Russian Songs. Nicolai Ghiaurov. Lon OS 26249

BOSSINENSIS, FRANCISCUS (fl ca 1500)
78   Haime per che m'ai Privo
      Album of Ayres. Donna Curry. Klav KS 513

BOUGHTON, RUTLAND (1878-
79   Faery song
      Ballads and Songs of Love and Sentiment. Stuart Burrows. Oiseau SOL 324

BOYCE, WILLAIM (1710-1779)
80   Momus to Mars
      Robert Tear sings Handel, Arne, Boyce, Hook. Argo ZRG 661

BRAHMS, JOHANNES (1833-1897)
81   Ach, Modr, ich well en Ding han
82   Ach, wende diesen Blick
83   Am Sonntag Morgen
      Brahms Songs. Elly Ameling. BASF KHB 21021
84   An eine Aeolsharfe
      German Lieder. Elisabeth Schumann. BWS SID 722
85   Auf dem Kirchhofe
      Heldentenor of the Century. Lauritz Melchior. 3-RCA CRM 3 0308
86   Bitteres zu sagen
87   Blinde Kuh
      German Lieder. Elisabeth Schumann. BWS SID 722
88   Botschaft
      Song Recital. Kathleen Ferrier. BWS 707
      Brahms Recital. Kathleen Ferrier. Rich R 23183
89   Da unten im Tale
90   Es steht ein' Lind in jenem Tal
      Brahms Songs. Elly Ameling. BASF KHB 21021
91   Es träumte mir
      Brahms Songs. Elly Ameling. BASF KHB 21021
      German Lieder. Elisabeth Schumann. BWS SID 722
92   Feinsliebchen, du sollst mir nicht barfuss geh'n
      Brahms Songs. Elly Ameling. BASF KHB 21021
93   Geistliches Wiegenlied (with viola)
94   Gestille Sehnsucht (with viola)
      Brahms Recital. Kathleen Ferrier. Rich R 23183
95   Immer leiser wird mein Schlummer
      Song Recital. Kathleen Ferrier. BWS 707
96   In stiller Nacht
      Brahms Songs. Elly Ameling. BASF KHB 21021
97   Der Jäger
      German Lieder. Elisabeth Schumann. BWS SID 722

98   Kein Haus, kein Heimat
     Recital. John Shirley-Quirk. Argo ZRG 664
99   Das Mädchen spricht
100   Mädchenlied (Auf die Nacht)
     Brahms Songs. Elly Ameling. BASF KHB 21021
101   Mein Herz ist schwer
102   Mit vierzig Jahren
     Recital. John Shirley-Quirk. Argo ZRG 664
103   Nachtigall
     German Lieder. Elisabeth Schumann. BWS SID 722
104   O kühler Wald
     Brahms Songs. Elly Ameling. BASF KHB 21021
105   Sapphische Ode
     Brahms Recital. Kathleen Ferrier. Rich R 23183
     Recital. John Shirley-Quirk. Argo ZRG 664
106   Die schöne Magelone (Keinen hat es noch gereut / Traun! Bogen und Pfeil sind
     gut für den Feind / Sind es Schmerzen, sind es Freuden / Liebe kam aus fernen
     Landen / So willst du des Armen / Wie soll ich die Freude / War es dir, dem diese
     Lippen bebten / Wir müssen uns trennen / Ruhe, Süssliebchen, im Schatten / So
     tönet denn, schäumende Wellen / Wie schnell verschwindet so Licht als Glanz /
     Muss es eine Trennung geben / Geliebter, wo zaudert dein irrender Fuss / Wie froh
     und frisch mein Sinn sich hebt / Treue Liebe dauert lange)
     Die schöne Magelone. Dietrich Fischer-Dieskau. Ang S 36753
     Die schöne Magelone. Bernard Kruysen. MHS 1377
107   Schwesterlein
     Brahms Songs. Elly Ameling. BASF KHB 21021
108   Sonntag
     Songs. John Stratton. Can 6236
109   Ständchen (Der Mond steht über dem Berge)
     Brahms Songs. Elly Ameling. BASF KHB 21021
110   Steig auf, geliebter Schatten
     Recital. John Shirley-Quirk. Argo ZRG 664
111   Der Tod das ist die kühle Nacht
     Song Recital. Kathleen Ferrier. BWS 707
112   Unbewegte, Laue Luft
     Brahms Songs. Elly Ameling. BASF KHB 21021
113   Vergebliches Ständchen
     Brahms Songs. Elly Ameling. BASF KHB 21021
     German Lieder. Elisabeth Schumann. BWS SID 722
114   Vier ernste Gesänge (Denn es gehet dem Menschen / Ich wandte mich / O Tod,
     wie bitter / Wenn ich mit Menschen)
     Brahms Recital. Kathleen Ferrier. Rich R 23183
     Recital. John Shirley-Quirk. Argo ZRG 664
115   Von ewiger Liebe
     Brahms Songs. Elly Ameling. BASF KHB 21021
     Song Recital. Kathleen Ferrier. BWS 707
116   Während des Regens
117   Wenn du nur zuweilen lächelst
     Brahms Songs. Elly Ameling. BASF KHB 21021
118   Wiegenlied
     German Lieder. Elisabeth Schumann. BWS SID 722

BRIDGE, FRANK (1879-1941)
119   Go not happy day
     Broadcast Recital of English Songs. Kathleen Ferrier. Rich R 23187
     Songs. John Stratton. Cant 6236

BRITTEN, BENJAMIN (1913-
120   The poet's echo (Russian) (Echo / My heart / Angel / The nightingale and the
rose / Epigram / Lines written during a sleepless night)
Britten and Tchaikowsky. Galina Vishnevskaya. Lon OS 26141

CACCINI, GIULIO (c.1545-1618)
121   Dolcissimo sospiro
Songs for Courtiers and Cavaliers. Helen Watts. Oiseau OLS 142

CADMAN, CHARLES WAKEFIELD (1881-1946)
122   At dawning
Ballads and Songs of Love and Sentiment. Stuart Burrows. Oiseau SOL 324

CALDARA, ANTONIO (1670-1736)
123   Cantata "La Rosa"
Concert. Beverly Sills. ABC ATS 20011
124   Sebben crudele
Italian Chamber Music. Dicran Jamgochian. Cor 2818

CALESTANI, VINCENZO (fl 1600)
125   Damigella tutta bella
126   Folgorate
Songs for Courtiers and Cavaliers. Helen Watts. Oiseau OLS 142

CAMPION, THOMAS (1567-1620)
127   It fell on a summer's day
128   Shall I come sweet love to thee?
129   Thy cypress curtain of the night
Elizabethan Lute Songs and Solos. Frank Patterson. Phi 6500282

CANTELOUBE, JOSEPH (1879-1957)
130   Songs of the Auvergne (Baïlèro / L'Aïo dè rotso / Ound'onerèn / Obal, din lou
Limouzi / La delaïssádo / Lo fiolaire / Passo pel prat / Brezairola / Chut, chut)
Canteloube and Chausson. Victoria de los Angeles. Ang S 36897

CAPEL, JOHN MAIS
131   Love, could I only tell thee
Ballads and Songs of Love and Sentiment. Stuart Burrows. Oiseau SOL 324

CARISSIMI, GIACOMO (1605-1676)
132   Vittoria, vittoria
Italian Chamber Music. Dicran Jamgochian. Cor 2818

CESTI, MARCANTONIO (1618-1669)
133   Languia già l'alba (Cantana)
Italian Cantatas of the 17th and Early 18th Centuries. Sylvia Stahlman.
Pleiades P 103

CHARLES, ERNEST (1895-
134   My lady walk'd in loveliness
Favorite American Concert Songs. Dale Moore. Can CRS 2715

CHAUSSON, ERNEST (1855-1899)
135 Poème de L'amour et de la mer (La fleur des eaux / Interlude / La mort de l'amour)
Canteloube and Chausson. Victoria de los Angeles. Ang S 36897

CHOPIN, FREDERIC (1810-1849)
136 Niema Czego Trzeba (Mélancholie)
137 Zyczenie (The maiden's wish)
A Tribute to Jennie Tourel. 2-Ody Y2 32880

CIFRA, ANTONIO (c.1575-c.1638)
138 In quel gelato core
Songs for Courtiers and Cavaliers. Helen Watts. Oiseau OLS 142

CIMARA, PIETRO (1887-1967)
139 Stornello
Tebaldi in Concert. Renata Tebaldi. Lon 26303

CLAY, FREDERIC (1838-1889)
140 I'll sing thee songs of Araby
Ballads and Songs of Love and Sentiment. Stuart Burrows. Oiseau SOL 324

COLERIDGE-TAYLOR, SAMUEL (1875-1912)
141 Eléanore
Ballads and Songs of Love and Sentiment. Stuart Burrows. Oiseau SOL 324

CORNELIUS, PETER (1824-1874)
142 Vaterunser (Vater unser / Geheiliget werde dein Name / Zu uns komme dein
Reich / Dein Wille geschehe / Unser täglich Brot gib uns heute / Vergib uns unsere
Schuld / Also auch wir vergeben unsern Schuldigern / Führe uns nicht in
Versuchung / Erlöse uns vom Übel)
143 Weihnachtslieder (Christbaum / Die Hirten / Die Könige / Simeon / Christus der
Kinderfreund / Christkind)
Cornelius. Hermann Prey. DG 2530108

CRUMB, GEORGE (1929-
144 Night of the four moons (La luna está muerta / Cuando sale la luna / Otro Adán
oscuro está sonando / Huje luna, luna, luna)
George Crumb. Jan De Gaetani. Col M 32739

CUMMING, RICHARD (1928-
145 Go, lovely rose
146 The little black boy
147 Memory, hither come
The Art Song in America, Vol. 2. John Hanks. Duke DWR 7306

DARGOMIZHSKY, ALEXANDER (1813-1869)
148 The old corporal (Russian)
149 A pleasant nocturnal breeze (Russian)
Russian Songs. Nicolai Ghiaurov. Lon OS 26249
150 Romance (Russian)
Jennie Tourel At Alice Tully Hall. Desto DC 7118-9
151 The worm (Russian)
Russian Songs. Nicolai Ghiaurov. Lon OS 26249

DAVIES, PETER MAXWELL (1934-
152   Eight songs for a mad king (The sentry / The country walk / The lady-in-waiting / To be sung on the water / The phantom queen / The counterfeit / Country dance / The review)
Peter Maxwell Davies. Julius Eastman. None H 71285

DEBUSSY, CLAUDE (1862-1918)
153   **Apparition**
Recital. Roberta Peters. BASF 20799
154   **Chansons de Bilitis (La flûte de Pan / La chevelure / Le tombeau des Naïades)**
French and Spanish Songs. Marilyn Horne. Lon OS 26301
Jennie Tourel at Alice Tully Hall. Desto DC 7118-9
A Tribute to Jennie Tourel. 2-Ody Y2 32880
155   **Clair de lune (1844)**
156   **Fêtes galantes I (En sourdine / Fantoches / Clair de lune)**
Recital. Roberta Peters. BASF 20799
157   **Fêtes galantes II (Les ingénus / Le faune / Colloque sentimental)**
Debussy Songs. Bernard Kruysen. Tel 22540
158   **Fleur des blés**
Recital. Roberta Peters. BASF 20799
159   **Noël des enfants qui n'ont plus de maisons**
Debussy Songs. Bernard Kruysen. Tel 22540
160   **Pierrot**
Recital. Roberta Peters. BASF 20799
161   **Le promenoir des deux amants (Auprès de cette grotte sombre / Crois mon conseil, chère Climène / Je tremble en voyant ton visage)**
Debussy Songs. Bernard Kruysen. Tel 22540
162   **Rondel chinois**
Recital. Roberta Peters. BASF 20799
163   **Trois ballades de Francois Villon (Ballade de Villon à s'amye / Ballade que Villon fait à la requeste de sa mère / Ballade des femmes de Paris)**
164   **Trois chansons de France (Le temps a laissié son manteau / La grotte / Pour ce que plaisance est morte)**
165   **Trois poèmes de Stéphane Mallarmé (Soupir / Placet futile / Eventail)**
Debussy Songs. Bernard Kruysen. Tel 22540

DELIBES, LEO (1836-1891)
166   **Les filles de Cadiz**
167   **Le rossignol**
Songs My Mother Taught Me. Joan Sutherland. Lon 26367

DEL RIEGO, TERESA
168   **Homing**
Songs My Mother Taught Me. Joan Sutherland. Lon 26367

DEL TREDICI, DAVID (1937-
169   **I hear an army**
Del Tredici, Diamond. Phyliss Bryn-Julson. CRI SD 294

D'INDIA, SIGISMONDO (c.1580-after 1627)
170   **Infelice didone**
171   **Torna il sereno zeffiro**
Songs for Courtiers and Cavaliers. Helen Watts. Oiseau OLS 142

DONIZETTI, GAETANO (1797-1848)
172   **A mezzanotte**
Romantic Songs. Lydia Marimpietri. Lon STS 15164

173   Amore e morte
174   Eterno amore e fè
     Romantic Songs. Ugo Benelli. Lon STS 15164
175   Me voglio fa 'na casa
     Romantic Songs. Lydia Marimpietri. Lon STS 15164
     Tebaldi in Concert. Renata Tebaldi. Lon 26303
176   Meine Liebe
     Romantic Songs. Lydia Marimpietri. Lon STS 15164

DOWLAND, JOHN (1562-1626)

177   Awake, sweet love
     Lute Songs and Dances. Hayden Blanchard. Orion 72102
     Dowland Songs and Dances. Hugues Cuenod. Turn 34510
     Elizabethan Lute Songs and Solos. Frank Patterson. Phi 6500282
178   Away with these self-loving lads
     Elizabethan Lute Songs and Solos. Frank Patterson. Phi 6500282
179   Can she excuse
     Lute Songs and Dances. Hayden Blanchard. Orion 72102
     Dowland Songs and Dances. Hugues Cuenod. Turn 34510
180   Come again, sweet love doth now invite
     Lute Songs and Dances. Hayden Blanchard. Orion 72102
     Dowland Songs and Dances. Hugues Cuenod. Turn 34510
     Elizabethan Lute Songs and Solos. Frank Patterson. Phi 6500282
181   Come away, come sweet love
     Lute Songs and Dances. Hayden Blanchard. Orion 72102
     Dowland Songs and Dances. Hugues Cuenod. Turn 34510
182   Come, heavy sleep
     Lute Songs and Dances. Hayden Blanchard. Orion 72102
183   Farewell, unkind
     Dowland Songs and Dances. Hugues Cuenod. Turn 34510
184   Fine knacks for ladies
     Dowland Songs and Dances. Hugues Cuenod. Turn 34510
     Elizabethan Lute Songs and Solos. Frank Patterson. Phi 6500282
185   Flow my tears
     Album of Ayres. Donna Curry. Klav KS 513
186   Fortune my foe
     Dowland Songs and Dances. Hugues Cuenod. Turn 34510
187   Go crystal tears
188   Go from my window
     Lute Songs and Dances. Hayden Blanchard. Orion 72102
189   I saw my lady weep
190   In darkness let me dwell
     Elizabethan Lute Songs and Solos. Frank Patterson. Phi 6500282
191   Now o now
     Dowland Songs and Dances. Hugues Cuenod. Turn 34510
192   Rest awhile you cruel cares
     Lute Songs and Dances. Hayden Blanchard. Orion 72102
193   Say, love, if ever thou did'st find
     Dowland Songs and Dances. Hugues Cuenod. Turn 34510
194   Shall I sue
     Elizabethan Lute Songs and Solos. Frank Patterson. Phi 6500282
195   Sorrow, sorrow, stay
196   Stay, time, awhile thy flying
     Dowland Songs and Dances. Hugues Cuenod. Turn 34510

DOWLAND, JOHN—*Continued*
197   Think'st thou then by thy feigning
        Lute Songs and Dances. Hayden Blanchard. Orion 72102
        Dowland Songs and Dances. Hugues Cuenod. Turn 34510
198   Weep you no more, sad fountains
        Dowland Songs and Dances. Hugues Cuenod. Turn 34510
199   What if I never speed
        Dowland Songs and Dances. Hugues Cuenod. Turn 34510
        Elizabethan Lute Songs and Solos. Frank Patterson. Phi 6500282
200   When Phoebus first did Daphne love
201   White as lilies was her face
        Dowland Songs and Dances. Hugues Cuenod. Turn 34510
202   Wilt thou, unkind, thus reave me
        Lute Songs and Dances. Hayden Blanchard. Orion 72102

DUKE, JOHN (1899-
203   I carry your heart
204   In just spring
205   Luke Havergal
206   The mountains are dancing
        The Art Song in America, Vol. 2. John Hanks. Duke DWR 7306

DURANTE, FRANCESCO (1684-1755)
207   Vergin tutt'amor
        Italian Chamber Music. Dicran Jamgochian. Cor 2818

DVORAK, ANTONIN (1841-1904)
208   Biblical songs (Czeck) (Clouds and darkness are round about / Lord, thou art
    my refuge / Hear my prayer, O Lord / God is my shepherd / I will sing Jehovah's
    praises / By the waters of Babylon / Turn thee to me / I will lift mine eyes to the
    mountain / Sing ye a joyful song)
209   I dreamed last night, Op. 3, No. 2 (Czech)
        Dvorak. Verá Soukupová. SUPRA ST 50898
210   Songs my mother taught me, Op. 55, No. 4
        Dvorak. Verá Soukupová. SUPRA ST 50898
        Songs My Mother Taught Me. Joan Sutherland. Lon 26367

EARLS, PAUL (1934-
211   Entreat me not to leave you
212   Love seeketh not itself to please
        The Art Song in America, Vol. 2. John Hanks. Duke DWR 7306

ELWELL, HERBERT (1898-
213   A child's grace
214   I look back
215   The ouselcock
216   Service of all the dead
217   This glittering grief
218   Wistful
        Elwell, Verrall, Walker. Maxine Makas. CRI SD 270

FALLA, MANUEL DE (1876-1946)
219 Seven popular Spanish songs (El pano moruno / Seguidilla murciana / Asturiana /
Jota / Nana / Canción / Polo)
The Concert at Hunter College. Victoria de los Angeles. Ang S 36896
French and Spanish Songs. Marilyn Horne. Lon OS 26301

FAURE, GABRIEL (1845-1924)
220 Accompagnement
221 Arpège
222 La Bonne Chanson (Une Sainte en son auréole / Puisque l'aube grandit / La lune
blanche luit dans les bois / J'allais par des chemins perfides / J'ai presque peur,
en vérité / Avant que tu ne t'en ailles / Donc, ce sera par un clair jour d'été)
Fauré Lieder. Bernard Kruysen. Tel 22546
223 Dans la forêt de Septembre
Fauré Lieder. Bernard Kruysen. Tel 22546
Fauré. Gérard Souzay. Phi 835286
224 Eau vivante
225 Exaucement
Fauré. Gérard Souzay. Phi 835286
226 La fleur qui va sur l'eau
Fauré Lieder. Bernard Kruysen. Tel 22546
Fauré. Gérard Souzay. Phi 835286
227 L'horizon chimérique (La mer est infinie / Je me suis embarqué / Diane, Séléné /
Vaisseaux, nous vous aurons aimée)
228 Je me poserai sur ton coeur
Fauré. Gérard Souzay. Phi 835286
229 Lydia
Recital. Stuart Burrows. Oiseau SOL 323
230 Madrigal
231 Mélodies de Venise (Mandoline / En sourdine / Green / A Clymène /
C'est l'extase)
Fauré. Gérard Souzay. Phi 835286
232 Mirages (Cygne sur l'eau / Reflets dans l'eau / Jardin nocturne/ Danseuse)
Fauré Lieder. Bernard Kruysen. Tel 22546
Fauré. Gérard Souzay. Phi 835286
233 Nell
Recital. Stuart Burrows. Oiseau SOL 323
234 O mort, poussière d'étoiles (La chanson d'Eve)
Fauré. Gérard Souzay. Phi 835286
235 Le parfum impérissable
Fauré Lieder. Bernard Kruysen. Tel 22546
236 Prison
Recital. Stuart Burrows. Oiseau SOL 323
237 La rose
Fauré. Gérard Souzay. Phi 835286
238 Sylvie
239 Toujours (Poèmes d'un jour)
Recital. Stuart Burrows. Oiseau SOL 323

FORD, THOMAS (1580-1648)
240 Since first I saw your face
Album of Ayres. Donna Curry. Klav KS 513

FOSTER, STEPHEN (1826-1864)
241 Ah! may the red rose live alway
Songs by Stephen Foster. Jan De Gaetani. None H 71268

FOSTER, STEPHEN—*Continued*
242   Beautiful dreamer
243   Gentle Annie
    Songs by Stephen Foster. Leslie Guinn. None H 71268
244   If you've only got a moustache
    Songs by Stephen Foster. Jan De Gaetani. None H 71268
245   I'm nothing but a plain old soldier
    Songs by Stephen Foster. Leslie Guinn. None H 71268
246   Jeanie with the light brown hair
247   Slumber my darling
    Songs by Stephen Foster. Jan De Gaetani. None. H 71268
248   Sweetly she sleeps, my Alice fair
249   There's a good time coming
    Songs by Stephen Foster. Leslie Guinn. None H 71268
250   Was my brother in the battle?
    Songs by Stephen Foster. Jan De Gaetani. None H 71268

FRANZ, ROBERT (1815-1892)
251   Auf dem Teich, dem regungslosen
252   Das ist ein Brausen und Heulen
253   Drüben geht die Sonne scheiden
254   Durch den Wald im Mondenscheine
255   Die Farben Helgolands
256   Der Fichtenbaum
257   Ein Friedhof
258   Frühlingsgedränge
259   Gewitternacht
260   Gute Nacht
261   Die helle Sonne leuchtet
262   Im Herbst
263   Im Rhein, im heiligen Strome
264   Die Lotosblume
265   Marie
266   Meeresstille
267   Romanze
268   Der Schalk
269   Sonnenuntergang, schwarze Wolken zieh'n
270   Trübe wird's, die Wolken jagen
271   Vergessen
272   Widmung
    Franz Songs. Peter Del Grande. EDUCO 4017

GALUPPI, BALDASSARE (1706-1785)
273   Se sapeste o giovinotti
    Bel Canto Arias. Peter Schreier. Tel SLT 43116

GASPARINI, FRANCESCO (1668-1727)
274   Lasciar d'amarti
    Italian Chamber Music. Dicran Jamgochian. Cor 2818
275   Primavera che tutt'amorosa
    Bel Canto Arias. Peter Schreier. Tel SLT 43116

GINÉNEZ Y BELLIDO, JERÓNIMO (1854-1923)
276   Zapateado
      The Concert at Hunter College. Victoria de los Angeles. Ang S 36896

GINASTERA, ALBERTO (1916-
277   Triste
      A Tribute to Jennie Tourel. 2-Ody Y2 32880

GLINKA, MIKHAIL (1804-1857)
278   Doubt
      Jennie Tourel at Alice Tully Hall. Desto DC 7118-9
279   The midnight review
      Russian Songs. Nicolai Ghiaurov. Lon OS 26249
280   Vain temptation
      Jennie Tourel at Alice Tully Hall. Desto DC 7118-9

GLOVER, CHARLES WILLIAM (1806-1863)
281   The rose of Tralee
      Ballads and Songs of Love and Sentiment. Stuart Burrows. Oiseau SOL 324

GLUCK, CHRISTOPH WILLIBALD (1714-1787)
282   O del mio dolce ardor
      Tebaldi in Concert. Renata Tebaldi. Lon 26303

GOUNOD, CHARLES (1818-1893)
283   Sérénade
      Songs My Mother Taught Me. Joan Sutherland. Lon 26367

GRANADOS, ENRIQUE (1867-1916)
284   Amor y odio
285   Callajeo
286   Gracia mía
287   Iban al pinar
288   Llorad, corazón
289   La maja de Goya
290   El majo discreto
291   El majo olvidado
292   El majo timido
293   Mananica era
294   Mira que soy nina
295   Il mirar de la maja
296   No lloreis, ojuelos
297   Las surrutacas modestas
298   El tra la la y el punteado
      The Concert at Hunter College. Victoria de los Angeles. Ang S 36896

GRANDI, ALLESANDRO (1575-1630)
299   Vientene, o mia crudel
      Songs for Courtiers and Cavaliers. Helen Watts. Oiseau OLS 142

GRIEG, EDVARD (1843-1907)
300   Eros
301   Ich liebe dich
      Heldentenor of the Century. Lauritz Melchior. 3-RCA CRM-3-0308
302   Solvejg's song
      Songs My Mother Taught Me. Joan Sutherland. Lon 26367

GRIEG, EDVARD—*Continued*
303   En Svane
Heldentenor of the Century. Lauritz Melchior. 3-RCA CRM-3-0308

GRIFFES, CHARLES TOMLINSON (1884-1920)
304   The lament of Ian the Proud
Favorite American Concert Songs. Dale Moore. Cam CRS 2715

HAGEMAN, RICHARD (1882-1966)
305   Do not go, my love
Favorite American Concert Songs. Dale Moore. Cam CRS 2715

HAHN, REYNALDO (1874-1947)
306   A Chloris
Songs. John Stratton. Cant 6236
307   Si mes vers avaient des alies
Songs My Mother Taught Me. Joan Sutherland. Col 26367
Jennie Tourel at Alice Tully Hall. Desto DC 7118-9

HANDEL, GEORGE FREDERIC (1685-1759)
308   Ah, che troppo inegali
Cantatas. Elly Ameling. 2-BASF 21687
309   Arm, arm ye brave (Judas Maccabaeus)
Handel Arias. Forbes Robinson. Argo ZRG 504
310   Cara sposa (Rinaldo)
Baroque—Sacred and Profane. Dietrich Fischer-Dieskau. Ang S-36904
311   Care selve (Atalanta)
Handel. Janet Baker. Phi 6500523
312   Deh lasciatemi il nemico (Tamerlano)
Handel. Carole Bogard. Cam CRS 2773
313   Dopo notte (Ariodante)
314   Dove sei, amato bene? (Rodelinda)
Handel. Janet Baker. Phi 6500523
315   The God of battle (Hercules)
316   Honour and arms (Samson)
Handel Arias. Forbes Robinson. Argo ZRG 504
317   How changed the vision (Admeto)
318   Like as the love-lorn turtle (Atalanta)
Broadcast Recital of English Songs. Kathleen Ferrier. Rich R 23187
319   Look down, harmonious saint (Praise of Harmony)
Cantatas. Theo Altmeyer. 2-BASF 21687
Robert Tear sings Handel, Arne, Boyce, Hook. Argo ZRG 661
320   Lucrezia
Handel. Janet Baker. Phi 6500523
Handel. Carole Bogard. Cam CRS 2773
321   Meine Seele hört im Sehen (Neun deutsche Arien)
Concert. Beverly Sills. ABC ATS 20011
Robert Tear sings Handel, Arne , Boyce, Hook. Argo ZRG 661
322   Nel dolce dell'oblio
Cantatas. Elly Ameling. 2-BASF 21687
323   O had I Jubal's lyre (Joshua)
Handel. Janet Baker. Phi 6500523
324   O ruddier than the cherry (Acis and Galatea)
Handel Arias. Forbes Robinson. Argo ZRG 504

325 Ombra mai fu (Serse)
    Handel. Janet Baker. Phi 6500523
326 Padre amato, in me riposa (Tamerlano)
    Handel. Carole Bogard. Cam CRS 2773
327 Peace crown'd with roses (Susanna)
328 Pensa a chi geme (Alcina)
329 Revenge, Timotheus cries (Alexander's Feast)
    Handel Arias. Forbes Robinson. Argo ZRG 504
330 Se non me vuol amar (Tamerlano)
    Handel. Carole Bogard. Cam CRS 2773
331 Se un bell'ardire (Ezio)
332 Si, tra i ceppi (Berenice)
    Handel Arias. Forbes Robinson. Argo ZRG 504
333 Silete venti
    Cantatas. Halina Lukomska. 2-BASF 21687
334 Süsse Stille (Neun deutsche Arien)
    Robert Tear sings Handel, Arne, Boyce, Hook. Argo ZRG 661
335 Waft her, angels (Jephtha)
    Recital. Stuart Burrows. Oiseau SOL 323
336 Where shall I fly? (Hercules)
    Handel. Janet Baker. Phi 6500523
337 Wide spread his mane (Theodora)
    Handel Arias. Forbes Robinson. Argo ZRG 504

HASSE, JOHANN ADOLPH (1699-1783)
338 Tradir sapeste, o perfidi (Arminio)
    Bel Canto Arias. Peter Schreier. Tel SLT 43116

HAYDN, FRANZ JOSEPH (1732-1809)
339 Abschiedslied
340 Auch die sprödeste der Schönen
341 Die zu späte Ankunft der Mutter
342 Fidelity
343 Gegenliebe
344 Geistliches Lied
345 Der Gleichsinn
346 Kaiserlied
347 Das Leben ist ein Traum
348 Lob der Faulheit
349 Piercing eyes
350 Recollection
351 Sailor's song
352 Eine sehr gewöhnliche Geschichte
353 She never told her love
354 The spirit's song
355 The wanderer
356 Zufriedenheit
    Songs. Dietrich Fischer-Dieskau. EMI Elec CO53-01 436

HOFHAIMER, PAUL (1459-1539)
357 Hertzliebstes Pild
    Album of Ayres. Donna Curry. Klav KS 513

HOMER, SIDNEY (1864-1953)
358 Requiem
    Songs. John Stratton. Cant 6236

HOMER, SIDNEY—*Continued*
359   The sick rose
      Favorite American Concert Songs. Dale Moore. Cam CRS 2715

HOOK, JAMES (1746-1827)
360   The lass of Richmond Hill
      Robert Tear sings Handel, Arne, Boyce, Hook. Argo ZRG 661

HOVHANESS, ALAN (1911-
361   Ararat
      Songs of Hovhaness. Ara Berberian. Pos S-1008
362   Black pool of cat
363   Dawn at Laona
      Songs by Alan Hovhaness. Ara Berberian. Pos 1005
364   Distant lake of sighs
      Songs of Hovhaness. Ara Berberian. Pos S-1009
365   Dulhey, Dulhey
366   The flute player of the Armenian Mountains (Kurd Isakin / Lalezar /
      Nachkhoonag / Sirds E Numan Mer Haireni Lerrneroon / Akh, Hoor E,
      Hoor E, Sirdus)
      Songs of Hovhaness. Ara Berberian. Pos S-1008
367   From high Armenia Mountain
      Songs of Hovhaness. Ara Bernerian. Pos S-1009
368   Gantznin Orern
369   Gurge Dikran
      Songs of Hovhaness. Ara Berberian. Pos S-1008
370   How I adore thee
      Songs by Alan Hovhaness. Ara Berberian. Pos 1005
371   In early dawn time
372   Live in the sun
      Songs of Hovhaness. Ara Berberian. Pos S-1009
373   Love songs of Hafiz
374   Lullaby of the lake
375   Out of the depths
      Songs by Alan Hovhaness. Ara Berberian. Pos 1005
376   Pagan saint
      Songs of Hovhaness. Ara Berberian. Pos S-1009
377   Three odes of Solomon
      Songs by Alan Hovhaness. Ara Berberian. Pos 1005
378   Two Shakespeare sonnets (When, in disgrace with fortune and men's eyes / When
      to the sessions of sweet silent thought)
379   Under a Byzantine dome
      Songs of Hovhaness. Ara Berberian. Pos S-1009

HUMMEL, JOHANN NEPOMUK (1778-1837)
380   Zur Logenfeier
      Frühe Goethe-Lieder. Dietrich Fischer-Dieskau. DG Archive 2533149

IVES, CHARLES (1874-1954)
381   Canon
382   Down east
383   Feldeinsamkeit
      Ives. Helen Boatwright. 4-Col M4 32504

384   In Flanders Field
        Ives. Thomas Stewart. 4-Col M4 32504
385   Incantation
386   Judges' walk
387   Luck and work
388   Mists
389   The new river
390   No more
391   Old home day
392   The one way
393   Peaks
394   Pictures
395   Requiem
396   Resolution
397   A sea dirge
398   The sea of sleep
399   September
400   The side show
401   Slow march
402   There is a certain garden
403   The things our fathers loved
404   West London
405   Widmung
406   Yellow leaves
        Ives. Helen Boatwright. 4-Col M4 32504

KANNE, FRIEDRICH AUGUST (1778-1833)
407   Des alten Abschied
408   Die Träume
        Das Wiener Lied um Schubert. Hermann Prey. DG Archive 2533123

KILPENIN, YRJO (1892-1959)
409   Jänkä
410   Kesäyö
411   Kirkkorannassa
412   Laululle
413   Rannalta I
414   Suvilaulu
415   Tunturille
416   Vanha kirkko
        A Lieder Recital. Martti Talvela. Lon 26240

KODALY, ZOLTAN (1882-1967)
417   A közelitö téls, Op. 5, No. 1
        Kodály Orchestral Songs. György Melis. Hung SLPX-11450
418   Imhol nyitva én kebelem, Op. 14, No. 2
        Kodály Orchestral Songs. József Simándy. Hung SLPX-11450
419   Kádár Kata (Hungarian folksong)
        Kodály Orchestral Songs. Márta Szirmay. Hung SLPX-11450
420   Mónár Anna (Hungarian folksong)
        Kodály Orchestral Songs. György Melis. Hung SLPX-11450
421   Siralmas nékem, Op. 14, No. 1
        Kodály Orchestral Songs. József Simándy. Hung SLPX-11450
422   Sirni, sirni, Op. 5, No. 2
        Kodály Orchestral Songs. György Melis. Hung SLPX-11450

28

KODALY, ZOLTAN—*Continued*
423　Várj meg madaram, Op. 14, No. 3
　　　Kodály Orchestral Songs. József Simándy. Hung SLPX-11450

KREUTZER, CONRADIN (1780-1849)
424　Ein Bettler vor dem Tor
　　　Frühe Goethe-Lieder. Dietrich Fischer-Dieskau. DG Archive 2533149
425　Frühlingsglaube
426　Wehmut
　　　Das Wiener Lied um Schubert. Hermann Prey. DG Archive 2533123

KRUFT, NIKOLAUS VON (1779-1818)
427　An Emma
　　　Das Wiener Lied um Schubert. Hermann Prey. DG Archive 2533123

LA FORGE, FRANK (1879-1953)
428　I came with a song
　　　Songs My Mother Taught Me. Joan Sutherland. Lon 26367

LASERNA, BLAS (1751-1816)
429　El Tripili
　　　The Concert at Hunter College. Victoria de los Angeles. Ang S-36896

LAWES, HENRY (1596-1662)
430　Among rosebuds
431　A complaint against Cupid
432　Dissuasion from presumption
433　An eccho
434　Hymn to God the Son
435　Hymn to God the Father
436　Hymn to God the Holy Ghost
437　I prithee send me back my heart
438　A lady to a young courtier
439　No constancy in man
440　Parting
441　Sufferance
442　Tavola In quel gelato core
　　　Songs for Courtiers and Cavaliers. Helen Watts. Oiseau OLS 142

LEO, LEONARDO (1694-1744)
443　Son qual nave in ria procella
　　　Bel Canto Arias. Peter Schreier. Tel SLT 43116

LESLIE, HENRY DAVID (1822-1896)
444　Annabelle Lee
　　　Ballads and Songs of Love and Sentiment. Stuart Burrows. Oiseau SOL 324

LISZT, FRANZ (1811-1886)
445　Benedetto sia'l giorno
　　　Sonnets of Petrarch. Dietrich Fischer-Dieskau. DG 2530332
446　"Comment" disaient-ils
　　　Jennie Tourel at Alice Tully Hall. Desto DC 7118-9
447　Du bist wie eine Blume
448　Es rauschen die Winde

449 Die Fischertochter
Liszt Songs. Peter Del Grande. EDUCO 4019
450 I'vidi in terra angelici costumi
Sonnets of Petrarch. Dietrich Fischer-Dieskau. DG 2530332
451 Kling' leise, mein Lied
452 Lasst mich ruhen
453 Die Lorelei
Liszt Songs. Peter Del Grande. EDUCO 4019
454 Mignons Lied
Liszt Songs. Peter Del Grande. EDUCO 4019
Jennie Tourel at Alice Tully Hall. Desto DC 7118-9
455 Nimm einen Strahl der Sonne
Liszt Songs. Peter Del Grande. EDUCO 4019
456 Oh! Quand je dors
Songs My Mother Taught Me. Joan Sutherland. Lon 26367
Jennie Tourel at Alice Tully Hall. Desto DC 7118-9
457 Pace non trovo
Sonnets of Petrarch. Dietrich Fischer-Dieskau. DG 2530332
458 Die stille Wasserrose
Liszt Songs. Peter Del Grande. EDUCO 4019
459 Über allen Gipfeln ist Ruh'
Jennie Tourel at Alice Tully Hall. Desto DC 7118-9
460 Und sprich
Liszt Songs. Peter Del Grande. EDUCO 4019
461 Vergiftet sind meine Lieder
Jennie Tourel at Alice Tully Hall. Desto DC 7118-9
462 Wieder möcht' ich dir begegnen
Liszt Songs. Peter Del Grande EDUCO 4019

LITERES, ANTONIO (c.1670-1747)
463 Confiado jilguerillo
The Concert at Hunter College. Victoria de los Angeles. Ang S-36896

LOEWE, KARL (1796-1867)
464 Tom der Reimer
Songs. John Stratton. Cant 6236

MACONCHY, ELIZABETH (1907-
465 Ariadne
Maconchy and Walton. Heather Harper. Oiseau SOL 331

MAHLER, GUSTAV (1860-1911)
466 Ablösung im Sommer
Mahler Songs. Dietrich Fischer-Dieskau. Col KM 30942
467 Blicke mir nicht in die Lieder
468 Ich atmet' einen linden Duft
Mahler Songs. Dietrich Fischer-Dieskau. Col KM 30942
Song Recital. Ljuba Welitsch. Ody Y 32675
469 Ich bin der Welt abhanden gekommen
Mahler Songs. Dietrich Fischer-Dieskau. Col KM 30942
Lieder Recital. Jessye Norman. Phi 6500412
Song Recital. Ljuba Welitsch. Ody Y 32675

MAHLER, GUSTAV—*Continued*
470   Das irdische Leben
     Mahler. Yvonne Minton. Lon OS 26195
     Mahler. Yvonne Minton. Lon CSA 2228
     Lieder Recital. Jessye Norman. Phi 6500412
471   Liebst du um Schönheit
     Lieder Recital. Jessye Norman. Phi 6500412
472   Lieder und Gesänge aus der Jugendzeit (Scheiden und meiden / Nicht Wiedersehen / Um schlimme Kinder artig zu machen / Frühlingsmorgen / Phantasie / Hans und Grete / Ich ging mit Lust durch einen grünen Wald / Starke Einbildungskraft / Erinnerung)
     Mahler, Schumann. Anna Reynolds. Oiseau S-327
473   Nicht Wiedersehen (Lieder und Gesänge aus der Jugendzeit) *See also* 472
     Mahler Songs. Dietrich Fischer-Dieskau. Col KM 30942
474   Rheinlegendchen (Des Knaben Wunderhorn)
     Mahler. Yvonne Minton. Lon OS 26195
     Mahler. Yvonne Minton. Lon CSA 2228
475   Scheiden und meiden (Lieder und Gesänge aus der Jugendzeit) *See also* 472
476   Selbstgefühl
477   Serenade aus "Don Juan"
478   Um Mitternacht
479   Um schlimme Kinder artig zu machen (Lieder und Gesänge aus der Jugendzeit) *See also* 472
     Mahler Songs. Dietrich Fischer-Dieskau. Col KM 30942
480   Urlicht
     Lieder Recital. Jessye Norman. Phi 6500412
481   Verlor'ne Müh (Des Knaben Wunderhorn)
     Mahler. Yvonne Minton. Lon OS 26195
     Mahler. Yvonne Minton. Lon CSA 2228
482   Wo die schönen Trompeten blasen (Des Knaben Wunderhorn)
     Mahler. Yvonne Minton. Lon OS 26195
     Mahler. Yvonne Minton. Lon CSA 2228
     Lieder Recital. Jessye Norman. Phi 6500412
483   Zu Strassburg auf der Schanz
     Mahler Songs. Dietrich Fischer-Dieskau. Col KM 30942

MAMLOK, URSULA (1928-
484   Stray birds (Stray birds / Let your music be like a sword / Tiny grass your steps are small)
     Rhodes, Smith, Ronsheim, Mamlok. Phyllis Bryn-Julson. CRI SD 301

MARCELLO, BENEDETTO (1686-1739)
485   Col pianto e coi sospiri
486   Latte e miele ecco vegg'io (Arianna)
     Bel Canto Arias. Peter Schreier. Tel SLT 43116

MARX, JOSEPH (1882-1964)
487   Hat dich die Liebe berührt
488   Valse de Chopin
     Song Recital. Ljuba Welitsch. Ody Y 32675

MASCAGNI, PIETRO (1863-1945)
489   Serenata
490   La tua stella
     Tebaldi in Concert. Renata Tebaldi. Lon 26303

MASSENET, JULES (1842-1912)
491   Crépuscule
       Songs My Mother Taught Me. Joan Sutherland. Lon 26367
492   Elegy
       Jennie Tourel at Alice Tully Hall. Desto DC 7118-9
493   Oh! Si les fleurs avaient des yeux
       Songs My Mother Taught Me. Joan Sutherland. Lon 26367

MAXWELL DAVIES, PETER *See* **DAVIES, PETER MAXWELL**

MEDTNER, NIKOLAI (1880-1951)
494   Alt Mütterlein, Op. 19, No. 2
495   Aus "Claudine von Villa-Bella", Op. 6, No. 5
       Medtner German Songs. Peter Del Grande. EDUCO 4016
496   Dawn, Op. 24, No. 7
497   Day and night, Op. 24, No. 1
498   The echo, Op. 31, No. 1
       Russian Songs. Peter Del Grande. Orion 7157
499   Einsamkeit, Op. 18, No. 3
       Medtner German Songs. Peter Del Grande. EDUCO 4016
500   Elegy, Op. 28, No. 5
501   Elegy, Op. 45, No. 1
       Russian Songs. Peter Del Grande. Orion 7157
502   Elfenliedchen, Op. 6, No. 3
503   Erster Verlust, Op. 6, No. 8
504   Ein Fichtenbaum, Op. 12, No. 2
505   Gefunden, Op. 6, No. 9
506   Geistergruss, Op. 15, No. 12
507   Geweihter Platz, Op. 46, No. 2
508   Gleich und gleich, Op. 15, No. 11
       Medtner German Songs. Peter Del Grande. EDUCO 4016
509   Heavy, empty and bleak, Op. 28, No. 4
       Russian Songs. Peter Del Grande. Orion 7157
510   Im Walde, Op. 46, No. 4
511   Lieb Liebchen, Op. 12, No. 1
512   Mailied, Op. 6, No. 2
513   Meeresstille, Op. 15, No. 7
       Medtner German Songs. Peter Del Grande. EDUCO 4016
514   Midday, Op. 61, No. 6
515   The muse, Op. 29, No. 1
       Russian Songs. Peter Del Grande. Orion 7157
516   Nachtgruss, Op. 61, No. 2
517   Praeludium, Op. 46, No. 1
       Medtner German Songs. Peter Del Grande. EDUCO 4016
518   The rose, Op. 29, No. 6
       Russian Songs. Peter Del Grande. Orion 7157
519   Selbstbetrug, Op. 15, No. 3
       Medtner German Songs. Peter Del Grande. EDUCO 4016
520   Signs, Op. 52, No. 4
521   Sleeplessness, Op. 37, No. 1
522   Spanish romance, Op. 52, No. 5
523   Twilight, Op. 24, No. 4
524   Verses written during insomnia, Op. 29, No. 3
       Russian Songs. Peter Del Grande. Orion 7157
525   Wanderers Nachtlied I, Op. 6, No. 1

MEDTNER, NIKOLAI— *Continued*
526   Wanderers Nachtlied II, Op. 15, No. 1
        Medtner German Songs. Peter Del Grande. EDUCO 4016
527   Waves and thoughts, Op. 24, No. 3
        Russian Songs. Peter Del Grande. Orion 7157
528   Winternacht, Op. 46, No. 5
        Medtner German Songs. Peter Del Grande. EDUCO 4016

MENDELSSOHN, FELIX (1809-1847)
529   Auf Flügeln des Gesanges
        Songs My Mother Taught Me. Joan Sutherland. Lon 26367

MERCADANTE, GIUSEPPE (1795-1870)
530   La sposa del marinaro
        Tebaldi in Concert. Renata Tebaldi. Lon 26303

MESSIAEN, OLIVER (1908-
531   Chants de terre et de ciel (Bail avec Mi / Antienne du silence / Danse du bébé-
        Pilule / Arc-en-ciel d'innocence / Minuit pile et face / Résurrection)
        Messiaen. Noelle Barker. Argo ZRG 699
532   Poèmes pour Mi (Action de grâces / Paysage / La maison / Epouvante / L'épouse /
        Ta voix / Les deux guerriers / Le collier / Prière exaucée)
        Messiaen. Noelle Barker. Argo ZRG 699
        Messiaen and Tippett. Felicity Palmer. Argo ZRG 703

METCALF, JOHN W. (1856-1926)
533   Absent
        Ballads and Songs of Love and Sentiment. Stuart Burrows. Oiseau SOL 324

MONRO, GEORGE (d. 1731)
534   My lovely Celia
        Ballads and Songs of Love and Sentiment. Stuart Burrows. Oiseau SOL 324

MONSIGNY, PIERRE ALEXANDRE (1729-1817)
535   La sagesse est un trésor
        Jennie Tourel at Alice Tully Hall. Desto DC 7118-9

MONTEVERDI, CLAUDIO (1567-1643)
536   Ecco pur ch'a voi ritorno
        Bel Canto Arias. Peter Schreier. Tel SLT 43116

MORLEY, THOMAS (1557-1602)
537   Come sorrow come
538   It was a lover and his lass
        Elizabethan Lute Songs and Solos. Frank Patterson. Phi 6500282
539   O mistress mine
        Album of Ayres. Donna Curry. Klav KS 513
540   Thyrsis and Milla
        Elizabethan Lute Songs and Solos. Frank Patterson. Phi 6500282

MOZART, WOLFGANG AMADEUS (1756-1791)
541   Abendempfindung K. 523
542   Ah, Spiegarti, Oh Dio K. 178
543   Als Luise die Briefe K. 520
544   Die Alte K. 517
        Mozart Lieder. Edith Mathis. DG 2530319

545 Bella mia fiamma, addio K. 528
     Mozart Soprano Arias. Jana Jonásová. Supra 1-12-1114
546 Chi sa, chi sa, qual sia K. 582
     Mozart Opera and Concert Arias. Elly Ameling. Phi 6500544
547 Con ossequio, con rispetto K. 210
     Concert Arias. József Réti. Hung 11485
548 Des kleinen Friedrichs Geburtstag K. 529
549 Der Frühling K. 597
550 Das Kinderspiel K. 598
551 Die kleine Spinnerin K. 531
     Mozart Lieder. Edith Mathis. DG 2530319
552 Mia speranza adorata K. 416
     Mozart Soprano Arias. Jana Jonásová. Supra 1-12-1114
553 Misera, dove son K. 369
     Mozart Opera and Concert Arias. Elly Ameling. Phi 6500544
554 Misero, o sogno, o son desto? K. 431
     Concert Arias. József Réti. Hung 11485
555 Un moto di gioia K.579
     Mozart Lieder. Edith Mathis. DG 2530319
556 No, no, che sei capace K. 419
     Mozart Soprano Arias. Jana Jonásová. Supra 1-12-1114
557 Oiseau, si tous les ans K. 307
     Mozart Lieder. Edith Mathis. DG 2530319
558 Per pietà, non ricercate K. 420
     Concert Arias. József Réti. Hung 11485
559 Popoli di Tessaglia. . .Io non chiedo, sterni Dei K. 300b
     Mozart Soprano Arias. Jana Jonásová. Supra 1-12-1114
560 Ridente la calma K. 152
     Mozart Lieder. Edith Mathis. DG 2530319
561 Schon lacht der holde Frühling K. 580
     Mozart Soprano Arias. Jana Jonásová. Supra 1-12-1114
562 Se al labbro mio non credi K. 295
     Concert Arias. József Réti. Hung 11485
563 Sehnsucht nach dem Frühlinge K. 596
564 Sei du mein Trost K. 391
     Mozart Lieder. Edith Mathis. DG 2530319
565 Si mostra la sorte K. 209
     Concert Arias. József Réti. Hung 11485
566 Vado, ma dove? K. 583
     Mozart Opera and Concert Arias. Elly Ameling. Phi 6500544
567 Das Veilchen K. 476
568 Die Verschweigung K. 518
569 Der Zauberer K. 472
570 Die Zufriedenheit K. 473
     Mozart Lieder. Edith Mathis. DG 2530319

MUDARRA, ALFONSO (16th Century)
571 Claro y Frescos Rios Si Uiesse e Me Leuasse
     Album of Ayres. Donna Curry. Klav KS 513

MUSSORGSKY, MODEST (1839-1881)
572 Songs and dances of death (Trepak / Lullaby / Serenade / The Field Marshal)
     Songs. Irina Arkhipova. Mel/Ang 40198
     A Tribute to Jennie Tourel. 2-Ody Y2 32880

NEEFE, CHRISTIAN GOTTLOB (1748-1798)
573   Serenate
Frühe Goethe-Lieder. Dietrich Fischer-Dieskau. DG Archive 2533149

NELSON, SYDNEY (1800-1862)
574   Mary of Argyle
Ballads and Songs of Love and Sentiment. Stuart Burrows. Oiseau SOL 324
Songs My Mother Taught Me. Joan Sutherland. Lon 26367

NEVIN, ETHELBERT (1862-1901)
575   The rosary
Ballads and Songs of Love and Sentiment. Stuart Burrows. Oiseau SOL 324

NIN, JOAQUIN (1879-1949)
576   Jesus de Nazareth
French and Spanish Songs. Marilyn Horne. Lon OS 26301
577   Pano Murciano
A Tribute to Jennie Tourel. 2-Ody Y2 32880
578   Villancico andaluz
579   Villancico asturiano
580   Villancico castellano
French and Spanish Songs. Marilyn Horne. Lon OS 26301

OBRADORS, FERNANDO J. (1897-1945)
581   Coplas de Curro Dulce
A Tribute to Jennie Tourel. 2-Ody Y2 32880

PARADISI, PIETRO DOMENICO (1710-1792)
582   M'ha presa alla sua regna
Tebaldi in Concert. Renata Tebaldi. Lon 26303

PARRY, CHARLES (1848-1918)
583   Love is a bable
Broadcast Recital of English Songs. Kathleen Ferrier. Rich R 23187

PERGOLESI, GIOVANNI BATTISTA (1710-1736)
584   Se tu m'ami
Tebaldi in Concert. Renata Tebaldi. Lon 26303

PERSICHETTI, VINCENT (1915-
585   The death of a soldier
586   The grass
587   Of the surface of things
588   The snow man
589   Thou child so wise
The Art Song in America, Vol. 2. John Hanks. Duke DWR 7306

PFITZNER, HANS (1869-1949)
590   Voll jener süsse
Sonnets of Petrarch. Dietrich Fischer-Dieskau. DG 2530332

PONCHIELLE, AMILCARE (1834-1886)
591   Non leggevamo insieme
      Tebaldi in Concert. Renata Tebaldi. Lon 26303

POULENC, FRANCIS (1899-1963)
592   Air romantique (Airs chantés)
593   Avant le cinéma
594   Cinq poèmes de Paul Eluard (Peut-il se reposer? / Il la prend dans ses bras / Plume
      d'eau claire / Rôdeuse au front de verre / Amoureuses)
595   Le grenouillère
596   Huit chansons polonaises (Polish) (La couronne / Le départ / Les gars polonaise /
      Le dernier Mazour / L'adieu / Le drapeau blanc / La Vistule / Le lac)
597   Nuages
598   Le travail du peintre (Pablo Picasso / Marc Chagall / Georges Braque / Juan Gris /
      Paul Klee / Joan Miró / Jacques Villon)
      Songs of Poulenc. Rose Dercourt. Turn 4489

PUCCINI, GIACOMO (1858-1924)
599   E l'uccelino
      Tebaldi in Concert. Renata Tebaldi. Lon 26303

PURCELL, HENRY (1658-1695)
600   Hark! the echoing air (The Faerie Queen)
601   Mad Bess of Bedlam
      Broadcast Recital of English Songs. Kathleen Ferrier. Rich R 23187

QUILTER, ROGER (1877-1953)
602   It was a lover and his lass
      Songs. John Stratton. Cant 6236
603   To Julia (Prelude / The bracelet / The maiden blush / To daisies / The night piece /
      Julia's hair / Interlude / Cherry ripe)
      Recital. Stuart Burrows. Oiseau SOL 323

RACHMANINOFF, SERGEI (1873-1943)
604   Although I beg you
      Rachmaninoff Songs. Peter Del Grande. EDUCO 4018
605   The answer, Op. 21, No. 4
      Rachmaninoff Songs. Nicolai Gedda. Ang S-36917
606   April, spring holiday
      Rachmaninoff Songs. Peter Del Grande. EDUCO 4018
607   Arion, Op. 34, No. 5
608   At my window
      Song Selections. Peter Del Grande. Orion 73109
      Rachmaninoff Songs. Nicolai Gedda. Ang S-36917
609   By my window *See* 608
610   Child, thou art fair as a flower, Op. 8, No. 2
      Songs. Irina Arkhipova. Mel/Ang 40198
611   Christ is risen, Op. 26, No. 6
      Rachmaninoff Songs. Nicolai Gedda. Ang S-36917
612   Day and night, Op. 34, No. 4
      Song Selections. Peter Del Grande. Orion 73109
      Rachmaninoff Songs. Nicolai Gedda. Ang S-36917

RACHMANINOFF, SERGEI— *Continued*

613   Do you have hiccups?

614   Don't leave me, Op. 4, No. 1
        Rachmaninoff Songs. Peter Del Grande. EDUCO 4018

615   A dream, Op. 8, No. 5
        Songs. Irina Arkhipova. Mel/Ang 40198

616   Extreme happiness, Op. 34, No. 12
        Song Selections. Peter Del Grande. Orion 73109

617   The floods of spring, Op. 14, No. 11
        Rachmaninoff Songs. Nicolai Gedda. Ang S-36917

618   The flower has wilted
        Rachmaninoff Songs. Peter Del Grande. EDUCO 4018

619   The fountain, Op. 26, No. 11
        Song Selections Peter Del Grande. Orion 73109

620   Fragment of Alfred de Musset, Op. 21, No. 6
        Songs. Irina Arkhipova. Mel/Ang 40198
        Rachmaninoff Songs. Nicolai Gedda. Ang S-36917

621   Harvest fields, Op. 4, No. 5
        Rachmaninoff Songs. Peter Del Grande. EDUCO 4018
        Rachmaninoff Songs. Nicolai Gedda. Ang S-36917

622   Harvest of sorrow   *See* **621**

623   How fair this spot, Op. 21, No. 7
        Rachmaninoff Songs. Nicolai Gedda. Ang S-36917

624   How long, my friend your sorrowful gaze, Op. 4, No. 6
        Rachmaninoff Songs. Peter Del Grande. EDUCO 4018

625   I remember that day, Op. 34, No. 10
        Song Selections. Peter Del Grande. Orion 73109
        Rachmaninoff Songs. Nicolai Gedda. Ang S-36917

626   I wait for thee, Op. 14, No. 1
        Songs. Irina Arkhipova. Mel/Ang 40198

627   I was with her, Op. 14, No. 4
        Song Selections. Peter Del Grande. Orion 73109

628   I will not tell you
        Rachmaninoff Songs. Peter Del Grande. EDUCO 4018

629   Impossible, Op. 34, No. 7

630   In my spirit, Op. 14, No. 10
        Song Selections. Peter Del Grande. Orion 73109

631   In the silence of the night, Op. 4, No. 3
        Songs. Irina Arkhipova. Mel/Ang 40198
        Rachmaninoff Songs. Peter Del Grande. EDUCO 4018
        Rachmaninoff Songs. Nicolai Gedda. Ang S-36917

632   In the silent and mysterious night   *See* **631**

633   In the silent night   *See* **631**

634   Lazarus has risen, Op. 34, No. 6
        Song Selections. Peter Del Grande. Orion 73109

635   Letter to K.S. Stanislavsky from S. Rachmaninoff
        Rachmaninoff Songs. Peter Del Grande. EDUCO 4018

636   Lilacs, Op. 21, No. 5
        Songs. Irina Arkhipova. Mel/Ang 40198
        Rachmaninoff Songs. Nicolai Gedda. Ang S-36917

637   Meditation, Op. 8, No. 3
        Rachmaninoff Songs. Peter Del Grande. EDUCO 4018

638   The morn of life   *See* **625**

639   The muse, Op. 34, No. 1

640   Music, Op. 34, No. 8
        Song Selections. Peter Del Grande. Orion 73109

641 Night
    Rachmaninoff Songs. Peter Del Grande. EDUCO 4018
642 O cease thy singing, maiden fair, Op. 4, No. 4
    Songs. Irina Arkhipova. Mel/Ang 40198
    Rachmaninoff Songs. Peter Del Grande. EDUCO 4018
    Rachmaninoff Songs. Nicolai Gedda. Ang S-36917
643 O, do not sing fair maiden *See* 642
644 Oh, do not grieve, Op. 14, No. 8
    Rachmaninoff Songs. Nicolai Gedda. Ang S-36917
645 Oh, never sing to me again *See* 642
646 Paid in full, Op. 34, No. 11
    Song Selections. Peter Del Grande. Orion 73109
647 The song of the disillusioned one
    Rachmaninoff Songs. Peter Del Grande. EDUCO 4018
648 The spirit is within us, Op. 34, No. 2
    Song Selections. Peter Del Grande. Orion 73109
649 The storm, Op. 34, No. 3
    Song Selections. Peter Del Grande. Orion 73109
    Rachmaninoff Songs. Nicolai Gedda. Ang S-36917
650 The tempest *See* 649
651 These summer nights, Op. 14, No. 5
    Song Selections. Peter Del Grande. Orion 73109
652 To the children, Op. 26, No. 7
653 Vocalise, Op. 34, No. 14
    Rachmaninoff Songs. Nicolai Gedda. Ang S-36917
654 Wind all around *See* 612
655 Yesterday we met, Op. 26, No. 13
656 You knew him, Op. 34, No. 9
    Song Selections. Peter Del Grande. Orion 73109

RAMEAU, JEAN PHILIPPE (1683-1764)
657 Thétis
    Baroque—Sacred and Profane. Dietrich Fischer-Dieskau. Ang S-36904

RAVEL, MAURICE (1875-1937)
658 Chansons Madécasses (Nahandove / Aoua / Il est doux de se coucher)
659 Vocalise
    A Tribute to Jennie Tourel. 2-Ody Y2 32880

REICHARDT, JOHANN FRIEDRICH (1752-1814)
660 An Lotte
    Frühe Goethe-Lieder. Dietrich Fischer-Dieskau. DG Archive 2533149
661 Canzon, s'al dolce loco
662 Di tempo in tempo
    Sonnets of Petrarch. Dietrich Fischer-Dieskau. DG 2530332
663 Einschränkung
664 Einziger Augenblick
    Frühe Goethe-Lieder. Dietrich Fischer-Dieskau. DG Archive 2533149
665 Erano i capei d'oro
    Sonnets of Petrarch. Dietrich Fischer-Dieskau. DG 2530332
666 Feiger Gedanken
667 Gott
668 Mut
    Frühe Goethe-Lieder. Dietrich Fischer-Dieskau. DG Archive 2533149
669 O poggi, o valli, o fiumi
670 Or ch'il ciel

REICHARDT, JOHANN FRIEDRICH—*Continued*
671   Più volte già dal bel sembiante
     Sonnets of Petrarch. Dietrich Fischer-Dieskau. DG 2530332
672   Rhapsodie
673   Die schöne Nacht
674   Tiefer liegt die Nacht um mich her
     Frühe Goethe-Lieder. Dietrich Fischer-Dieskau. DG Archive 2533149

RHODES, PHILLIP (1940-
675   Autumn setting (Autumn fragments / Prophecy / Remembrance / Reality)
     Rhodes, Smith, Ronsheim, Mamlok. Phyllis Bryn-Julson. CRI SD 301

RICCI, FEDERICO (1809-1877)
676   Il carretiere del Vomero
     Tebaldi in Concert. Renata Tebaldi. Lon 26303

RIMSKY-KORSAKOV, NIKOLAI (1844-1908)
677   An angel is flying through the midnight sky, Op. 40, No. 2
678   Conjuring
679   The echo, Op. 27, No. 2
680   From my tears my little one, there were many fragrant flowers born, Op. 2, No. 4
681   The golden cloud slept, Op. 3, No. 3
682   I awaited you in the grotto, Op. 40, No. 4
683   In the dark bouquet, the nightingale fell silent, Op. 4, No. 3
684   The messenger, Op. 4, No. 2
685   The nightingale's infatuation with the rose, Op. 2, No. 2
686   The pine tree and the palm, Op. 3, No. 1
687   Place your cheek against mine, Op. 2, No. 1
688   The secret, Op. 8, No. 3
689   Silence descends on the yellow fields, Op. 39, No. 4
690   The soul flew softly through the heavens, Op. 27, No. 1
691   There, where you are, my thoughts are flying, Op. 8, No. 1
692   Upon the hills of Georgia, Op. 3, No. 8
693   What good will be my name to you?, Op. 4, No. 1
694   When waves the yellowing field of corn, Op. 40, No. 1
695   Zuleika's song, Op. 26, No. 4
     Rimsky-Korsakov Songs. Peter Del Grande. EDUCO 4020

ROGERS, JAMES H. (1857-1940)
696   The time for making songs has come
     Favorite American Concert Songs. Dale Moore. Cam CRS 2715

RONSHEIM, JOHN RICHARD (1927-
697   Bitter-sweet
698   Easter-wings
     Rhodes, Smith, Ronsheim, Mamlok. Jan De Gaetani. CRI SD 301

ROREM, NED (1923-
699   A Christmas carol
700   Clouds
701   For Susan
702   Guilt
703   What sparks and wiry cries
     The Art Song in America, Vol. 2. John Hanks. Duke DWR 7306

ROSA, SALVATOR (1615-1673)
704   Vado ben spesso cangiando loco
       Italian Chamber Music. Dicran Jamgochian. Cor 2818

ROSSETER, PHILIP (c.1575-1623)
705   Sweet come again
706   What then is love but mourning
707   Whether men do laugh or weep
       Elizabethan Lute Songs and Solos. Frank Patterson. Phi 6500282

ROSSI, LUIGI (1597-1653)
708   Horche l'oscuro manto (cantata)
       Italian Cantatas of the 17th and Early 18th Centuries. Sylvia Stahlman.
       Pleiades P 103

ROSSINI, GIOACCHINO (1792-1868)
709   La gita in gondola
       Romantic Songs. Ugo Benelli. Lon STS 15164
710   L'invito-bolero
       Tebaldi in Concert. Renata Tebaldi. Lon 26303
711   L'orgia
712   La partenza
       Romantic Songs. Lydia Marimpietri. Lon STS 15164
713   L'ultimo ricordo
       Italian Chamber Music. Dicran Jamgochian. Cor 2818

RUBINSTEIN, ANTON (1829-1894)
714   Melody
       Russian Songs. Nicolai Ghiaurov. Lon OS 26249

SACHSEN-WEIMAR, ANNA AMALIE VON (1723-1787)
715   Auf dem Land und in der Stadt
716   Sie scheinen zu spielen
       Frühe Goethe-Lieder. Dietrich Fischer-Dieskau. DG Archive 2533149

SANDERSON, WILFRED (1878-
717   Until
       Ballads and Songs of Love and Sentiment. Stuart Burrows. Oiseau SOL 324

SATIE, ERIK (1866-1925)
718   Le chapelier
719   Je te veux
       A Tribute to Jennie Tourel. 2-Ody Y2 32880

SCARLATTI, ALESSANDRO (1660-1725)
720   Al fin m'ucciderete (cantata)
       Italian Cantatas of the 17th and Early 18th Centuries. Sylvia Stahlman.
       Pleiades P 103
721   Gia il sole dal Gange
       Songs. John Stratton. Cant 6236
722   O cessate di piagarmi
       Tebaldi in Concert. Renata Tebaldi. Lon 26303
723   Rugiadose, adorose *See* 726

SCARLATTI, ALESSANDRO— *Continued*
724   Sento nel core
    Recital. Stuart Burrows. Oiseau SOL 323
    Italian Chamber Music. Dicran Jamgochian. Cor 2818
725   Son tutta duolo
    Recital. Stuart Burrows. Oiseau SOL 323
726   Le violette
    Recital. Stuart Burrows. Oiseau SOL 323
    Bel Canto Arias. Peter Schreier. Tel SLT 43116

SCHOENBERG, ARNOLD (1874-1951)
727   Two songs, Op. 1 (Dank / Abschied)
    Complete Songs, Vol. 1. Donald Gramm. 2-Col M31311/2
728   Four songs, Op. 2 (Erwartung / Jesus bettelt / Erhebung / Waldsonne)
    Complete Songs, Vol. 1. Ellen Faull. 2-Col M31311/2
729   Six songs, Op. 3 (Wie Georg von Frundsberg von sich selber sang / Die
    Aufgeregten / Warnung / Hochzeitslied / Geübtes Herz / Freihold)
    Complete Songs, Vol. 2. Donald Gramm (1) Helen Vanni (2-6)
    2-Col M31311/2
730   Eight songs, Op. 6 (Traumleben / Alles / Mädchenlied / Verlassen / Ghasel /
    Am Wegrand / Lockung / Der Wanderer)
    Complete Songs, Vol. 2. Helen Vanni. 2-Col M31311/2
731   Two ballads, Op. 12 (Jane Grey / Der verlorene Haufen)
    Complete Songs, Vol. 2. Cornelius Opthof. 2-Col M31311/2
732   Two songs, Op. 14 (Ich darf nicht dankend / In diesen Wintertagen)
    Complete Songs, Vol. 2. Helen Vanni. 2-Col M31311/2
733   Das Buch der hängenden Gärten, Op. 15 (Unterm Schutz von dichten
    Blättergründen / Hain in diesen Paradiesen / Als Neuling trat ich ein in dein
    Gahege / Da meine Lippen reglos sind und brennen / Saget mir, auf welchen
    Pfade / Jedem Werke bin ich fürder tot / Angst und Hoffen wechselnd mich
    beklemenn / Wenn ich heut nicht deinen Leib berühre / Streng ist uns das Glück
    und spröde / Das schöne Beet betracht ich mir im Harren / Als wir hinter dem
    beblümten Tore / Wenn sich bei heiliger Ruh / Du lehnest wider eine Silberweide /
    Sprich nicht immer / Wir bevölkerten die abend-düstern)
    Complete Songs, Vol. 1. Helen Vanni. 2-Col M31311/2
734   Three songs, Op. 48 (Sommermüd / Tot / Mädchenlied)
735   Two songs, Op. (Posthumous) (Gedenken / Am Strande)
    Complete Songs, Vol. 2. Helen Vanni. 2-Col M31311/2
736   Die Aufgeregten, Op. 3, No. 2 *See also* 729
737   Erwartung, Op. 2, No. 1 *See also* 728
738   Geübtes Herz, Op. 3, No. 5 *See also* 729
739   Ich darf nicht dankend, Op. 14, No. 1 *See also* 732
740   Sommermüd, Op. 48, No. 1 *See also* 734
741   Tot, Op. 48, No. 2 *See also* 734
742   Verlassen, Op. 6, No. 4 *See also* 730
    Songs of the New Vienna School. Dietrich Fischer-Dieskau. DG 2530107

SCHUBERT, FRANZ (1797-1828)
743   Abendstern D. 806
    Schubert Lieder. Dietrich Fischer-Dieskau. DG 2530347
744   Allein, nachdenklich, gelähmt D. 629
    Sonnets of Petrarch. Dietrich Fischer-Dieskau. DG 2530332
745   Am Bach im Frühling D. 361
    Lieder. Christa Ludwig. DG 2530404
746   Am See D. 746
    Schubert Songs. Dietrich Fischer-Dieskau. DG 2530347

747 An den Frühling D. 245
     Schiller Lieder. Dietrich Fischer-Dieskau. DG 2530306
748 An den Mond D. 259
749 An den Mond D. 296 (Version II)
     Schubert Lieder to Goethe Texts. Dietrich Fischer-Dieskau. DG 2530229
750 An die Freude D. 189
     Schiller Lieder. Dietrich Fischer-Dieskau. DG 2530306
751 An die Musik D. 547
     Lieder Recital. Kathleen Ferrier. Rich R 23184
     Schubert and Schumann. Hermann Prey. Phi 6520002
752 An die Nachtigall D. 497
     Janet Baker sings Schubert. 2-Sera S-6083
     Lieder. Christa Ludwig. DG 2530404
753 An die untergehende Sonne D. 457
     Janet Baker sings Schubert. 2-Sera S-6083
754 An Sylvia D. 891
     Schubert and Schumann. Hermann Prey. Phi 6520002
755 Apollo, lebet noch dein hold Verlangen D. 628
     Sonnets of Petrarch. Dietrich Fischer-Dieskau. DG 2530332
756 Auf dem Wasser zu singen D. 774
     Schubert and Schumann. Hermann Prey. Phi 6520002
757 Auf der Donau D. 553
     Lieder. Christa Ludwig. DG 2530404
758 Auflösung D. 807
     Schubert Lieder. Dietrich Fischer-Dieskau. DG 2530347
759 Berthas Lied in der Nacht D. 653
     Janet Baker sings Schubert. 2-Sera S-6083
760 Der blinde Knabe D. 833b
     Schubert Lieder. Dietrich Fischer-Dieskau. DG 2530347
761 Die Bürgschaft D. 246
     Schiller Lieder. Dietrich Fischer Dieskau. DG 2530306
762 Delphine D. 857
     Janet Baker sings Schubert. 2-Sera S-6083
763 Des Mädchens Klage D. 191
     Janet Baker sings Schubert. 2-Sera S-6083
     Lieder. Christa Ludwig. DG 2530404
764 Du bist die Ruh' D. 776
     Recital. Stuart Burrows. Oiseau SOL 323
     Song Recital. Kathleen Ferrier. BWS 707
765 Du liebst mich nicht D. 756
     Song Recital. Kathleen Ferrier. BWS 707
766 Ellens erster Gesang (Raste, Krieger) D. 837
767 Ellens zweiter Gesang (Jäger, ruhe von der Jagd) D. 838
     Janet Baker sings Schubert. 2-Sera S-6083
     Lieder Recital. Jessye Norman. Phi 6500412
768 Ellens dritter Gesang (Ave Maria) D. 839
     Janet Baker sings Schubert. 2-Sera S-6083
     Lieder. Christa Ludwig. DG 2530404
     Lieder Recital. Jessye Norman. Phi 6500412
769 Frühlingsglaube D. 686
     Lieder. Christa Ludwig. DG 2530404
770 Erlkönig D. 328
     Schubert Lieder to Goethe Texts. Dietrich Fischer-Dieskau. DG 2530229
     Goethe Songs. Hermann Prey. Phi 6500515
771 Der Fischer D. 225
     Schubert Lieder to Goethe Texts. Dietrich Fischer-Dieskau. DG 2530229

SCHUBERT, FRANZ—*Continued*

772 **Die Forelle D. 550**
Schubert and Schumann. Hermann Prey. Phi 6500002

773 **Ganymed D. 544**
Goethe Songs. Hermann Prey. Phi 6500515

774 **Das Geheimnis D. 250**
Schiller Lieder. Dietrich Fischer-Dieskau. DG 2530306

775 **Gesänge des Harfners D. 478, 479, 480 (Wer sich der Einsamkeit ergibt / An die Türen will ich schleichen / Wer nie sein Brot mit Tränen ass)**
Schubert Lieder to Goethe Texts. Dietrich Fischer-Dieskau. DG 2530229
Goethe Songs. Hermann Prey. Phi 6500515

776 **Die Götter Griechenlands D. 677**
Schiller Lieder. Dietrich Fischer-Dieskau. DG 2530306

777 **Grablied D. 218**
Schubert Lieder. Dietrich Fischer-Dieskau. DG 2530347

778 **Gretchen am Spinnrade D. 118**
Janet Baker sings Schubert. 2-Sera S-6083
Lieder Recital. Kathleen Ferrier. Rich R 23184
Lieder. Christa Ludwig. DG 2530404

779 **Gruppe aus dem Tartarus D. 583**
Schiller Lieder. Dietrich Fischer-Dieskau. DG 2530306

780 **Heidenröslein D. 257**
Goethe Songs. Elly Ameling. Phi 6500515
Recital. Stuart Burrows. Oiseau SOL 323
Schubert Lieder to Goethe Texts. Dietrich Fischer-Dieskau. DG 2530229

781 **Herrn Joseph Spaun D. 749**
Janet Baker sings Schubert. 2-Sera S-6083
Schubert Lieder. Dietrich Fischer-Dieskau. DG 2530347

782 **Hin und wieder (Claudine von Villa Bella) D. 239**
Janet Baker sings Schubert. 2-Sera S-6083

783 **Der Hirt auf dem Felsen D. 965**
Concert. Beverly Sills. ABC ATS 20011

784 **Im Abendrot D. 799**
Lieder. Christa Ludwig. DG 2530404

785 **Im Haine D. 738**
Schubert Songs. Dietrich Fischer-Dieskau. DG 2530347

786 **Iphigenia D. 573**
Janet Baker sings Schubert. 2-Sera S-6083

787 **Die junge Nonne D. 828**
Janet Baker sings Schubert. 2-Sera S-6083
Song Recital. Kathleen Ferrier. BWS 707
Lieder Recital. Kathleen Ferrier. Rich R 23184
Lieder. Christa Ludwig. DG 2530404

788 **Der Jüngling am Bache D. 638**
Schiller Lieder. Dietrich Fischer-Dieskau. DG 2530306

789 **Der Jüngling auf dem Hügel D. 702**

790 **Der Jüngling und der Tod D. 545**

791 **Der Knabe in der Wiege D. 579b**
Schubert Lieder. Dietrich Fischer-Dieskau. DG 2530347

792 **Der König in Thule D. 367**
Lieder. Christa Ludwig. DG 2530404

793 **Lachen und Weinen D. 777**
Lieder. Christa Ludwig. DG 2530404
Schubert and Schumann. Hermann Prey. Phi 6500002

794 **Leiden der Trennung D. 509**
Schubert Songs. Dietrich Fischer-Dieskau. DG 2530347

795 **Liebe schwärmt** D. 239
Janet Baker sings Schubert. 2-Sera S-6083
796 **Die Liebende schreibt** D. 673
797 **Liebhaber in allen Gestalten** D. 558
Goethe Songs. Elly Ameling. Phi 6500515
798 **Lied der Mignon (Kennst du das Land?)** D. 321
799 **Lied der Mignon (Heiss mich nicht reden)** D. 877
800 **Lied der Mignon (So lasst mich scheinen)** D. 877
Goethe Songs. Elly Ameling. Phi 6500515
Janet Baker sings Schubert. 2-Sera S-6083
801 **Lied der Mignon (Nur wer die Sehnsucht kennt)** D. 877
Goethe Songs. Elly Ameling. Phi 6500515
Janet Baker sings Schubert. 2-Sera S-6083
Lieder. Christa Ludwig. DG 2530404
802 **Lied eines Schiffers an die Dioskuren** D. 360
Schubert and Schumann. Hermann Prey. Phi 6500002
803 **Das Mädchen aus der Fremde** D. 252
Schiller Lieder. Dietrich Fischer-Dieskau. DG 2530306
804 **Die Männer sind méchant** D. 866/3
Janet Baker sings Schubert. 2-Sera S-6083
805 **Meeres Stille** D. 216
Schubert Lieder to Goethe Texts. Dietrich Fischer-Dieskau. DG 2530229
806 **Der Musensohn** D. 764
Lieder Recital. Kathleen Ferrier. Rich R 23184
807 **Nachtgesang** D. 119
Schubert Lieder to Goethe Texts. Dietrich Fischer-Dieskau. DG 2530229
808 **Nähe des Geliebten** D. 162
Goethe Songs. Elly Ameling. Phi 6500515
Schubert Lieder to Goethe Texts. Dietrich Fischer-Dieskau. DG 2530229
809 **Der Neugierige (Die schöne Müllerin)** D. 795 *See also* 818
Recital. Stuart Burrows. Oiseau SOL 323
810 **Nunmehr, da Himmel, Erde schweigt** D. 630
Sonnets of Petrarch. Dietrich Fischer-Dieskau. DG 2530332
811 **Der Pilgrim** D. 794
Schiller Lieder. Dietrich Fischer-Dieskau. DG 2530306
812 **Rastlose Liebe** D. 138
Schubert Lieder to Goethe Texts. Dietrich Fischer-Dieskau. DG 2530229
813 **Romanze aus Rosamunde** D. 797
Song Recital. Kathleen Ferrier. BWS 707
Lieder. Christa Ludwig. DG 2530404
814 **Die Rose** D. 745
Lieder. Christa Ludwig. DG 2530404
815 **Der Sänger** D. 149
Schubert Lieder to Goethe Texts. Dietrich Fischer-Dieskau. DG 2530229
Goethe Songs. Hermann Prey. Phi 6500515
816 **Schäfers Klagelied** D. 121
Schubert Lieder to Goethe Texts. Dietrich Fischer-Dieskau. DG 2530229
817 **Schlummerlied** D. 527
Janet Baker sings Schubert. 2-Sera S-6083
818 **Die schöne Müllerin** D. 795 (Das Wandern / Wohin / Halt / Dangsagung an den Bach / Am Feierabend / Der Neugierige / Ungeduld / Morgengruss / Des Müllers Blumen / Tränenregen / Mein / Pause / Mit dem grünen Lautenbande / Der Jäger / Eifersucht und Stolz / Die liebe Farbe / Die böse Farbe / Trock'ne Blumen / Der Müller und der Bach / Des Baches Wiegelied)
Lieder, Vol. III. Dietrich Fischer-Dieskau. 4-DG 2720059
Die schöne Müllerin. Hermann Prey. Lon 26251

SCHUBERT, FRANZ—*Continued*

819   Schwanengesang **D. 957** (Liebesbotschaft / Kriegers Ahnung / Frühlingssehnsucht / Ständchen / Aufenthalt / In der Ferne / Abschied / Der Atlas / Ihr Bild / Das Fischermädchen / Die Stadt / Am Meer / Der Doppelgänger / Die Taubenpost)
Lieder, Vol. III. Dietrich Fischer-Dieskau. 4-DG 2720059
Schwanengesang. Tom Krause. Lon OS-26328

820   Schwestergruss **D. 762**
Janet Baker sings Schubert. 2-Sera S-6083
Lieder Recital. Jessye Norman. Phi 6500412

821   Sehnsucht **D. 123**
Schiller Lieder. Dietrich Fischer-Dieskau. DG 2530306

822   Der Strom **D. 565**
Schubert Lieder. Dietrich Fischer-Dieskau. DG 2530347

823   Suleika I **D. 720**
824   Suleika II **D. 717**
Janet Baker sings Schubert. 2-Sera S-6083

825   Der Tod und das Mädchen **D. 531**
Song Recital. Kathleen Ferrier. BWS 707
Lieder. Christa Ludwig. DG 2530404

826   Totengrabers Heimweh **D. 842**
827   Der Vater mit dem Kind **D. 906**
Schubert Lieder. Dietrich Fischer-Dieskau. DG 2530347

828   Der Wanderer **D. 649**
829   Der Wanderer an den Mond **D. 870**
Schubert and Schumann. Hermann Prey. Phi 6520002

830   Wanderers Nachtlied **D. 224**
Schubert Lieder to Goethe Texts. Dietrich Fischer-Dieskau. DG 2530229

831   Wehmut **D. 772**
Schubert Lieder. Dietrich Fischer-Dieskau. DG 2530347

832   Wiegenlied **D. 498**
833   Wiegenlied **D. 867**
Janet Baker sings Schubert. 2-Sera S-6083

834   Die Winterreise **D.911** (Gute Nacht / Die Wetterfahne / Gefror'ne Tränen / Erstarrung / Der Lindenbaum / Wasserfluth / Auf dem Flusse / Rückblick / Irrlicht / Rast / Frühlingstraum / Einsamkeit / Die Post / Der greise Kopf / Die Krähe / Letzte Hoffnung / Im Dorfe / Der stürmische Morgen / Täuschung / Der Wegweiser / Das Wirtshaus /Muth/ Die Nebensonnen / Der Leiermann)
Lieder, Vol. III. Dietrich Fischer-Dieskau. 4-DG 2720059
Die Winterreise. Hermann Prey. Phi 6747033

835   Der zürnende Barde **D. 785**
Schubert Songs. Dietrich Fischer-Dieskau. DG 2530347

836   Der Zwerg **D. 771**
Schubert Songs. Dietrich Fischer-Dieskau. DG 2530347
Lieder Recital. Jessye Norman. Phi 6500412

SCHUMANN, ROBERT (1810-1856)

837   Aufträge, **Op. 77, No. 5**
Lieder. Elly Ameling. BASF 26369
Schumann and Wolf Lieder. Harold Enns. Orion 74146

838   Aus den östichen Rosen, **Op. 25, No. 25** *See also* **869**
Schumann and Wolf Lieder. Harold Enns. Orion 74146

839   Belsazar, **Op. 57**
Schumann and Wolf Lieder. Harold Enns. Orion 74146
Les Lieder de 1840. Bernard Kruysen. 6-Val CMB 17

840   Dichterliebe, Op. 48 (Im wunderschönen Monat Mai / Aus meinen Tränen spriessen / Die Rose, die Lilie / Wenn ich in deine Augen seh / Ich will meine Seele tauchen / Im Rhein, im heiligen Strome / Ich grolle nicht / Und wüsstens die Blumen / Das ist ein Flöten und Geigen / Hör ich das Liedchen klingen / Ein Jüngling liebt ein Mädchen / Am leuchtenden Sommermorgen / Ich hab im Traum geweinet / Allnächtlich im Träume / Aus alten Märchen / Die alten, bösen Lieder)

    Les Lieder de 1840. Bernard Kruysen. 6-Val CMB 17

    Schubert and Schumann. Hermann Prey. Phi 6520002

841   Er ist's, Op. 79, No. 23

    Lieder. Elly Ameling. BASF 26369

    German Lieder. Elisabeth Schumann. BWS SID-722

842   Erstes Grün, Op. 35, No. 4 (Kerner Lieder) *See also* **847**

    Lieder. Elly Ameling. BASF 26369

    Schumann and Wolf Lieder. Harold Enns. Orion 74146

843   Frage, Op. 35, No. 9 (Kerner Lieder) *See also* **847**

    Lieder. Elly Ameling. BASF 26369

844   Frauenliebe und Leben, Op. 42 (Seit ich ihn gesehen / Er, der Herrlichste von allen / Ich kanns nicht fassen / Du Ring an meinem Finger / Helft mir, ihr Schwestern / Süsser Freund, du blickest / An meinem Herzen / Nun hast du mir den ersten Schmerz getan)

    Schumann and Wagner. Kathleen Ferrier. DIS 3700

    Song Recital. Kathleen Ferrier. BWS 707

    Lieder Recital. Kathleen Ferrier. Rich R 23184

    Les Lieder de 1840. Danielle Galland. 6-Val CMB 17

    German Lieder. Elisabeth Schumann. BWS SID-722

845   Freisinn, Op. 25, No. 2 (Myrthen) *See also* **869**

    Schumann and Wolf Lieder. Harold Enns. Orion 74146

846   Gedichte, Op. 30 (Der Knabe mit dem Wunderhorn / Der Page / Der Hidalgo)

    Les Lieder de 1840. Bernard Kruysen. 6-Val CMB 17

847   Gedichte, Op. 35 (Kerner Lieder) (Lust der Sturmnacht / Stirb, Lieb' und Freud / Wanderlied / Erstes Grün / Sehnsucht nach der Waldgegend / Auf das Trinkglas eines verstorbenen Freundes / Wanderung / Stille Liebe / Frage / Stille Tränen / Wer machte dich so krank / Alte Laute)

    Les Lieder de 1840. Danielle Galland and Bernard Kruysen. 6-Val CMB 17

    Schumann. Gérard Souzay. Odeon 163-11325

    A Lieder Recital. Martti Talvela. Lon 26240

848   Gedichte, Op. 36 (Sonntags am Rhein / Ständchen / Nichts Schöneres / An den Sonnenschein / Dichters Genesung / Liebesbotschaft)

    Les Lieder de 1840. Bernard Kruysen. 6-Val CMB 17

849   Gesänge, Op. 31 (Die Löwenbraut / Die Kartenlegerin / Die rothe Hanne)

    Les Lieder de 1840. Danielle Galland and Bernard Kruysen. 6-Val CMB 17

850   Hochländers Abschied, Op. 25, No. 13 (Myrthen) *See also* **869**

    Schumann and Wolf Lieder. Harold Enns. Orion 74146

851   Ihre Stimme, Op. 96, No. 3

    Schumann. Gérard Souzay. Odeon 163-11325

852   Jasminenstrauch, Op. 27, No. 4 *See also* **859**

    Lieder. Elly Ameling. BASF 26369

    Schumann and Wolf Lieder. Harold Enns. Orion 74146

853   Die Kartenlegerin, Op. 31, No. 2 *See also* **849**

854   Das Käuzlein, Op. 79, No. 10

    Lieder. Elly Ameling. BASF 26369

855   Kerner Lieder *See* **847**

856   Die letzten Blumen starben, Op. 104, No. 6

    Lieder. Elly Ameling. BASF 26369

SCHUMANN, ROBERT—*Continued*

857   Liebesfrühling, Op. 37 (Der Himmel hat eine Träne geweint / O ihr Herren / Ich hab' in mich gesogen / Liebste, was kann denn uns scheiden / Flügel, Flügel, um zu fliegen / Rose, Meer und Sonne / O Sonn', O Meer, O Rose)

858   Lieder, Op. 40 (Märzveilchen / Muttertraum / Der Soldat / Der Spielmann / Verratene Liebe)

859   Lieder und Gesänge I, Op. 27 (Sag' an, o lieber Vogel mein / Dem roten Röslein gleicht mein Lieb / Was soll ich sagen / Jasminenstrauch / Nur ein lächelnder Blick)
        Les Lieder de 1840. Danielle Galland and Bernard Kruysen. 6-Val CMB 17

860   Lieder und Gesänge II, Op. 51 (Sehnsucht / Volksliedchen / Ich wand're nicht / Auf dem Rhein / Liebeslied)
        Les Lieder de 1840. Danielle Galland. 6-Val CMB 17

861   Liederkreis, Op. 24 (Morgens steh' ich auf und frage / Es treibt mich hin / Ich wandelte unter den Bäumen / Lieb' Liebchen, leg's Händchen / Schöne Wiege meiner Leiden / Warte, warte, wilder Schiffsmann / Berg' und Burgen schau'n herunter / Anfangs wollt' ich fast verzagen / Mit Myrthen und Rosen)
        Les Lieder de 1840. Bernard Kruysen. 6-Val CMB 17
        Schumann. Robert Tear. Argo ZRG 718

862   Liederkreis, Op. 39 (In der Fremde / Intermezzo / Waldesgespräch / Die Stille / Mondnacht / Schöne Fremde / Auf einer Burg / In der Fremde / Wehmut / Zwielicht / Im Walde / Frühlingsnacht)
        Les Lieder de 1840. Bernard Kruysen. 6-Val CMB 17
        Mahler and Schumann. Anna Reynolds. Oiseau S-327
        Schumann. Robert Tear. Argo ZRG 718

863   Loreley, Op. 53, No. 2 *See also* 875

864   Marienwürmchen, Op. 79, No. 13

865   Die Meerfee, Op. 125, No. 3
        Lieder. Elly Ameling. BASF 26369

866   Mein schöner Stern, Op. 101, No. 4
        Lieder. Elly Ameling. BASF 26369
        Schumann. Gérard Souzay. Odeon 163-11325

867   Meine Rose, Op. 90, No. 2
        Schumann and Wolf Lieder. Harold Enns. Orion 74146

868   Mondnacht (Liederkreis, Op. 39) *See also* 862
        German Lieder. Elisabeth Schumann. BWS SID-722

869   Myrthen, Op. 25 (Widmung / Freisinn / Der Nussbaum / Jemand / Sitz' ich allein / Setze mir nicht / Die Lotusblume / Talismane / Lied der Suleika / Die Hochländer-Witwe / Mutter, Mutter / Lass mich ihm am Busen hangen / Hochländers Abschied / Hochländisches Wiegenlied / Aus den hebräischen Gesängen / Rätsel / Leis' rudern hier / Wenn durch die Piazzetta / Hauptmann's Weib / Weit, weit / Was will die einsame Träne / Niemand / Im Westen / Du bist wie eine Blume / Ich sende einen Gruss / Zum Schluss)
        Les Lieder de 1840. Danielle Galland and Bernard Kruysen. 6-Val CMB 17

870   Nachtlied, Op. 96, No. 1
        Schumann. Gérard Souzay. Odeon 163-11325

871   Der Nussbaum, Op. 25 *See also* 869

872   O ihr Herren, Op. 37, No. 3 *See also* 857
        German Lieder. Elisabeth Schumann. BWS SID-722

873   Romanzen und Balladen I, Op. 45 (Der Schatzgräber / Frühlingsfahrt / Abends am Strand)

874   Romanzen und Balladen II, Op. 49 (Die beiden Grenadiere / Die feindlichen Brüder / Die Nonne)

875   Romanzen und Balladen III, Op. 53 (Blondels Lied / Loreley / Der arme Peter I, II, III)
        Les Lieder de 1840. Bernard Kruysen. 6-Val CMB 17

876 Röselein, Op. 89, No. 6
    German Lieder. Elisabeth Schumann. BWS SID-722
877 Der Sandman, Op. 79, No. 12
878 Schmetterling, Op. 79, No. 2
    Lieder. Elly Ameling. BASF 26369
879 Schneeglöckchen, Op. 79, No. 26
    Lieder. Elly Ameling. BASF 26369
    German Lieder. Elisabeth Schumann. BWS SID-722
    Schumann. Gérard Souzay. Odeon 163-11325
880 Sehnsucht, Op. 51, No. 1 *See also* 860
881 Sehnsucht nach der Waldgegend, Op. 35, No. 5 (Kerner Lieder) *See also* 847
882 Die Sennin, Op. 90, No. 4
    Lieder. Elly Ameling. BASF 26369
883 Ständchen, Op. 36, No. 2 *See also* 848
    German Lieder. Elisabeth Schumann. BWS SID-722
884 Volksliedchen, Op. 51, No. 2 *See also* 860
    Lieder Recital. Kathleen Ferrier. Rich R 23184
885 Waldesgespräch, Op. 39, No. 3 (Liederkreis) *See also* 862
    Lieder. Elly Ameling. BASF 26369
886 Widmung, Op. 25, No. 1 *See also* 869
    Lieder. Elly Ameling. BASF 26369
    Lieder Recital. Kathleen Ferrier. Rich R 23184
    Schumann. Gérard Souzay. Odeon 163-11325
887 Zwei venetianische Lieder, Op. 25, No. 17, 18 (Leis' rudern hier / Wenn durch
die Piazzetta *See also* 869
    Schumann. Gérard Souzay. Odeon 163-11325

SECKENDORFF, SIEGMUND VON (1744-1785)
888 Romanze
    Frühe Goethe-Lieder. Dietrich Fischer-Dieskau. DG Archive 2533149

SENFL, LUDWIG (c.1490-1543)
889 Ach Elselein liebes Elselein mein
890 Die Weyber mit den Flohen
    Album of Ayres. Donna Curry. Klav KS 513

SERMISY, CLAUDIN DE (c.1490-1562)
891 Secourses moy, tant que vivray
    Album of Ayres. Donna Curry. Klav KS 513

SIBELIUS, JEAN (1865-1957)
892 Svarta Rosor
    Heldentenor of the Century. Lauritz Melchior. 3-RCA CRM-3-0308
    Songs. John Stratton. Cant 6236

SMITH, HALE (1925-
893 Envoy in autumn
894 Spring
895 The valley wind
896 Velvet shoes
    Rhodes, Smith, Ronsheim, Mamlok. Hilda Harris. CRI SD 301

SPEAKS, OLEY (1875-1948)
897 On the Road to Mandalay
    Favorite American Concert Songs. Dale Moore. Cam CRS 2715

SPONTINI, GASPARO (1774-1851)
898   Bien peu de chose
899   Il faut helas
     Italian Chamber Music. Dicran Jamgochian. Cor 2818

STANFORD, C. VILLERS (1852-1924)
900   The Fairy Lough
901   A soft day
     Broadcast Recital of English Songs. Kathleen Ferrier. Rich R 23187

STEFFANI, AGOSTINO (1654-1724)
902   A facile vittoria (Tassilone)
903   Piangerete, io ben io so (Tassilone)
     Bel Canto Arias. Peter Schreier. Tel SLT 43116

STILLMAN-KELLEY, EDGAR (1857-1944)
904   Eldorado
     Favorite American Concert Songs. Dale Moore. Cam CRS 2715

STRADELLA, ALESSANDRO (c.1645-1682)
905   A quel candido foglio (cantata)
     Italian Cantatas of the 17th and Early 18th Centuries. Sylvia Stahlman.
     Pleiades P 103
906   Aria di chiesa
     Italian Chamber Music. Dicran Jamgochian. Cor 2818
907   Per pietà
     Jennie Tourel at Alice Tully Hall. Desto DC 7118-9

STRAUSS, RICHARD (1864-1949)
908   All mein Gedanken, Op. 21, No. 1
     Recital. Roberta Peters. BASF 20799
     Songs by Strauss and Korngold. Lea Piltti. Roc 5350
909   Als mir dein Lied erklang, Op. 68, No. 4
910   Amor, Op. 68, No. 5
     Recital. Roberta Peters. BASF 20799
911   Breit über mein Haupt, Op. 19, No. 2
     Songs by Strauss and Korngold. Anton Dermota. Roc 5350
912   Cäcilie, Op. 27, No. 2
     Heldentenor of the Century. Lauritz Melchior. 3-RCA CRM-3-0308
     Songs by Strauss and Korngold. Maria Reining. Roc 5350
     Song Recital. Ljuba Welitsch. Ody Y 32675
913   Du meines Herzens Krönelein, Op. 21, No. 2
     Songs by Strauss and Korngold. Anton Dermota. Roc 5350
914   Four last songs (Frühling / September / Beim Schlafengehen / Im Abendrot)
     Song Recital. Ljuba Welitsch. Ody Y 32675
915   Freundliche Vision, Op. 48, No. 1
     Songs by Strauss and Korngold. Maria Reining. Roc 5350
916   Heimkehr, Op. 15, No. 5
     Songs by Strauss and Korngold. Lea Piltti. Roc 5350
917   Heimliche Aufforderung, Op. 27, No. 3
     Songs by Strauss and Korngold. Anton Dermota. Roc 5350
     Heldentenor of the Century. Lauritz Melchior. 3-RCA CRM-3-0308
918   Ich liebe dich, Op. 37, No. 2
     Songs by Strauss and Korngold. Anton Dermota. Roc 5350

919   **Ich schwebe, Op. 48, No. 2**
     Recital. Roberta Peters. BASF 20799
     Songs by Strauss and Korngold. Lea Piltti. Roc 5350

920   **Ich trage meine Minne, Op. 32, No. 1**
     Songs by Strauss and Korngold. Anton Dermota. Roc 5350

921   **Kling, Op. 48, No. 3**
     Songs by Strauss and Korngold. Lea Piltti. Roc 5350

922   **Meinem Kinde, Op. 37, No. 3**
     Songs by Strauss and Korngold. Maria Reining. Roc 5350

923   **Morgen, Op. 27, No. 4**
     Recital. Roberta Peters. BASF 20799

924   **Die Nacht, Op. 10, No. 3**
     Songs by Strauss and Korngold. Anton Dermota. Roc 5350
     Song Recital. Ljuba Welitsch. Ody Y 32675

925   **Säusle, liebe Myrte, Op. 68, No. 3**
     Recital. Roberta Peters. BASF 20799

926   **Schlagende Herzen, Op. 29, No. 2**
     Songs by Strauss and Korngold. Lea Piltti. Roc 5350

927   **Seitden dein Aug', Op. 17, No. 1**
     Songs by Strauss and Korngold. Anton Dermota. Roc 5350

928   **Ständchen, Op. 17, No. 2**
     Recital. Roberta Peters. BASF 20799
     Songs by Strauss and Korngold. Lea Piltti. Roc 5350

929   **Traum durch die Dämmerung, Op. 29, No. 1**
     Heldentenor of the Century. Lauritz Melchior. 3-RCA CRM-3-0308
     Songs by Strauss and Korngold. Maria Reining. Roc 5350

930   **Waldseligkeit, Op. 49, No. 1**
     Songs by Strauss and Korngold. Maria Reining. Roc 5350

931   **Zueignung, Op. 10, No. 1**
     Songs by Strauss and Korngold. Anton Dermota. Roc 5350
     Heldentenor of the Century. Lauritz Melchior. 3-RCA CRM-3-0308
     Songs by Strauss and Korngold. Maria Reining. Roc 5350
     Songs. John Stratton. Cant 6236

SULLIVAN, ARTHUR (1842-1900)

932   **The lost chord**
     Ballads and Songs of Love and Sentiment. Stuart Burrows. Oiseau SOL 324

TCHAIKOVSKY, PETER ILYITCH (1840-1893)

933   **Again, as before, Op. 73, No. 6**

934   **As over hot embers, Op. 25, No. 2**
     Tchaikovsky Songs. Robert Tear. Argo ZRG 707

935   **At the ball, Op. 38, No. 3**
     Songs. Peter Del Grande. Orion 74156
     Russian Songs. Nicolai Ghiaurov. Lon OS 26249
     Tchaikovsky Songs. Robert Tear. Argo ZRG 707
     Britten and Tchaikovsky. Galina Vishnevskaya. Lon OS 26141

936   **Cradle song, Op. 16, No. 1**
     Tchaikovsky Songs. Robert Tear. Argo ZRG 707

937   **Darkness has fallen, Op. 47, No. 3**

938   **Day is reigning, Op. 47, No. 6**

939   **A dead man's love, Op. 38, No. 5**
     Songs. Peter Del Grande. Orion 74156

TCHAIKOVSKY, PETER ILYITCH— *Continued*

940   Disappointment, Op. 65, No. 2
941   Do not believe me, my dear, Op. 6, No. 1
942   Do not leave me, Op. 27, No. 3
        Tchaikovsky Songs. Robert Tear. Argo ZRG 707
943   Don Juan's serenade, Op. 38, No. 1
        Songs. Peter Del Grande. Orion 74156
        Russian Songs. Nicolai Ghiaurov. Lon OS 26249
        Tchaikovsky Songs. Robert Tear. Argo ZRG 707
944   Evening, Op. 27, No. 4
        Songs. Peter Del Grande. Orion 74156
945   Fearful moment, Op. 28, No. 6
        Songs. Peter Del Grande. Orion 74156
        Tchaikovsky Songs. Robert Tear. Argo ZRG 707
946   Florentine song, Op. 38, No. 6
        Songs. Peter Del Grande. Orion 74156
947   Great deeds, Op. 60, No. 11
        Tchaikovsky Songs. Robert Tear. Argo ZRG 707
948   I bless you forests, Op. 47, No. 5
        Songs. Peter Del Grande. Orion 74156
        Russian Songs. Nicolai Ghiaurov. Lon OS 26249
949   In the clamour of the ballroom *See* 935
950   It was in the early spring, Op. 38, No. 2
        Songs. Peter Del Grande. Orion 74156
        Russian Songs. Nicolai Ghiaurov. Lon OS 26249
951   Look, yonder floats, Op. 27, No. 2
        Songs. Peter Del Grande. Orion 74156
952   Mid the din of the ball *See* 935
953   Mignon's song *See* 960
954   My genius, my angel, my friend; Reconcilement, Op. 25, No. 1
955   My little minx, Op. 27, No. 6
        Tchaikovsky Songs. Robert Tear. Argo ZRG 707
956   Neither an answer, Op. 28, No. 5
        Songs. Peter Del Grande. Orion 74156
957   Night, Op. 73, No. 2
        Britten and Tchaikovsky. Galina Vishnevskaya. Lon OS 26141
958   No answer, no word, no greeting *See* 945
959   No, I will never name, Op. 28, No. 1
        Songs. Peter Del Grande. Orion 74156
960   None but the lonely heart, Op. 6, No. 6
        Russian Songs. Nicolai Ghiaurov. Lon OS 26249
        Tchaikovsky Songs. Robert Tear. Argo ZRG 707
        Jennie Tourel at Alice Tully Hall. Desto DC 7118-9
961   Not a word, O my friend, Op. 6, No. 2
        Russian Songs. Nicolai Ghiaurov. Lon OS 26249
962   O, if you only could, Op. 38, No. 4
        Songs. Peter Del Grande. Orion 74156
963   O stay, Op. 16, No. 2
        Tchaikovsky Songs. Robert Tear. Argo ZRG 707
964   On the golden cornfields, Op. 57, No. 2
965   Serenade, Op. 63, No. 6
        Britten and Tchaikovsky. Galina Vishnevskaya. Lon OS 26141
966   That was in early springtime *See* 950
967   They kept on saying "you fool", Op. 25, No. 6
968   Through the window, Op. 60, No. 10

969   To forget so soon, is it not so?, **Op. 16, No. 5**
        Tchaikovsky Songs. Robert Tear. Argo ZRG 707

970   Why, **Op. 6, No. 5**

971   Why did I dream of you?, **Op. 28, No. 3**
        Britten and Tchaikovsky. Galina Vishnevskaya. Lon OS 26141

TELEMANN, GEORG PHILIPP (1681-1767)

972   Ihr Völker, hört
        Baroque—Sacred and Profane. Dietrich Fischer-Dieskau. Ang S-36904

973   Non ho più core (Der geduldige Sokrates)
        Bel Canto Arias. Peter Schreier. Tel SLT 43116

TEYBER, ANTON (1754-1822)

974   Liebesschmerz
        Das Wiener Lied um Schubert. Hermann Prey. DG Archive 2533123

TIPPETT, MICHAEL (1905-

975   Songs for Dov (I was born in a big town / Know you the land where the lemon
        bushes flower? / I passed by their home)
        Messiaen and Tippett. Robert Tear. Argo ZRG 703

TOMASCHEK, WENZEL JOHANN (1774-1850)

976   Abendlied

977   An den Mond

978   An Linna

979   Rastlose Liebe

980   Schäfers Klagelied

981   Selbstbetrug

982   Trost in Tränen

983   Wanderers Nachtlied
        Das Wiener Lied um Schubert. Hermann Prey. DG Archive 2533123

TORELLI, GIUSEPPE (1658-1709)

984   Tu lo sai
        Italian Chamber Music. Dicran Jamgochian. Cor 2818

TOSELLI, ENRICO (1883-1926)

985   Serenata
        Ballads and Songs of Love and Sentiment. Stuart Burrows. Oiseau SOL 324

TOSTI, F. PAOLO (1846-1916)

986   My dreams
        Ballads and Songs of Love and Sentiment. Stuart Burrows. Oiseau SOL 324

987   Sogno
        Tebaldi in Concert. Renta Tebaldi. Lon 26303

TRIMBLE, LESTER (1923-

988   Love seeketh not itself to please

989   Tell me where is fancy bred?
        The Art Song in America, Vol. 2. John Hanks. Duke DWR 7306

TROMBONCINO, BARTOLOMEO (fl.1487-1514)

990   Poi che volse la mia stella
        Album of Ayres. Donna Curry. Klav KS 513

VAUGHAN WILLIAMS, RALPH (1872-1958)
991   Linden Lea
992   Orpheus with his lute
      Songs by Vaughan Williams. Robert Tear. Argo ZRG 732
993   Silent noon
      Broadcast Recital of English Songs. Kathleen Ferrier. Rich R 23187
994   Songs of travel (The vagabond / Bright is the ring of words / The roadside fire)
995   Ten Blake songs for voice and oboe (Infant Joy / A poison tree / The piper /
      London / The lamb / The shepherd / Ah! sunflower / Cruelty has a human heart /
      The divine image / Eternity)
      Songs by Vaughan Williams. Robert Tear. Argo ZRG 732

VERDI, GIUSEPPE (1813-1901)
996   Brindisi
      Italian Chamber Music. Dicran Jamgochian. Cor 2818

VILLA-LOBOS, HEITOR (1887-1959
997   Cancao Do Carreiro
      A Tribute to Jennie Tourel. 2-Ody Y2-32880

WAGNER, RICHARD (1813-1883)
998   Branders Lied
999   Lied des Mephistopheles
      Frühe Goethe-Lieder. Dietrich Fischer-Dieskau. DG Archive 2533149
1000   Schmerzen (Wesendonck Lieder) *See also* 1002
1001   Träume (Wesendonck Lieder) *See also* 1002
      Heldentenor of the Century. Lauritz Melchior. 3-RCA CRM-3-0308
1002   Wesendonck Lieder (Der Engel / Stehe still / Im Treibhaus / Schmerzen / Träume)
      Schumann and Wagner. Kirsten Flagstad. DIS 3700

WALTON, WILLIAM (1902-
1003   Daphne
1004   Old Sir Faulk
1005   A song for the Lord Mayor's table (The Lord Mayor's table / Glide gently /
      Wapping old stairs / Holy Thursday / The contrast / Rhyme)
1006   Through gilded trellises
      Maconchy and Walton. Heather Harper. Oiseau SOL 331

WARLOCK, PETER (1894-1930)
1007   Pretty ring-time
1008   Sleep
      Broadcast Recital of English Songs. Kathleen Ferrier. Rich R 23187

WEBERN, ANTON (1883-1945)
1009   Am Ufer
1010   An Baches Ranft
1011   Bild der Liebe
1012   Dies ist ein Lied
1013   Gefunden
1014   Ihr tratet zu dem Herde
1015   Noch zwingt mich treue
1016   So ich traurig bin
1017   Vorfrühling
      Songs of the New Vienna School. Dietrich Fischer-Dieskau. DG Archive 2530107

WEIGL, KARL (1881-1949)
1018 Beatrix
Karl Weigl Songs. George Shirley. Turn 34522
1019 Blaue Nacht
1020 Es goss mein volles Leben
Karl Weigl Songs. Betty Allen. Turn 34522
1021 Five Lieder aus "Phantasus" (Aus weissen Wolken baut sich ein Schloss / Dann losch das Licht / Über die Welt hin ziegen die Wolken / In meinem schwarzen Taxuswald / Auf einem vergoldeten Blumenschiff)
Karl Weigl Songs. Judith Raskin. Turn 34522
1022 Halleluja der Sonne
Karl Weigl Songs. William Warfield. Turn 34522
1023 Liebeslied
1024 Lied der Schiffermädels
Karl Weigl Songs. Betty Allen. Turn 34522
1025 Lieder der Liebe und Einsamkeit (Der Einsamste / Der Tage klingt ab / Schmied Schmerz)
1026 O Nacht, du silberbleiche
Karl Weigl Songs. William Warfield. Turn 34522
1027 Schlummerlied
1028 Seele
Karl Weigl Songs. George Shirley. Turn 34522
1029 Spielmannslied
Karl Weigl Songs. Betty Allen. Turn 34522
1030 Das unsichtbare Licht
Karl Weigl Songs. George Shirley. Turn 34522
1031 Wiegenlied
Karl Weigl Songs. William Warfield. Turn 34522

WILLIAMS, W. S. GWYNN (1896-
1032 My little Welsh home
Ballads and Songs of Love and Sentiment. Stuart Burrows. Oiseau SOL 324

WOLF, HUGO (1860-1903)
1033 Auf ein altes Bild (Mörike) *See also* **1046**
Lieder Recital. Kathleen Ferrier. Rich R 23184
Cornelius and Wolf. Hermann Prey. DG 2530108
1034 Auf einer Wanderung (Mörike) *See also* **1046**
Lieder Recital. Kathleen Ferrier. Rich R 23184
1035 Biterolf (von Scheffel)
Lieder von Hugo Wolf. Dietrich Fischer-Dieskau. 7-Odeon 181 01470/76
1036 Drei Gedichte von Michelangelo (Wohl denk ich oft / Alles endet, was entstehet / Fühlt meine Seele das ersehnte Licht von Gott)
Schumann and Wolf Lieder. Harold Enns. Orion 74146
Lieder von Hugo Wolf. Dietrich Fischer-Dieskau. 7-Odeon 181 01470/76
1037 Eichendorff Lieder (Selections) (Erwartung / Der Freund / Der Glücksritter / Heimweh / In der Fremde I / Lieber alles / Liebesglück / Der Musikant / Nachruf / Die Nacht / Nachtzauber / Der Scholar / Der Schreckenberger / Seemanns Abschied / Der Soldat I, II / Das Ständchen / Umfall / Verschwiegene Liebe / Der verzweifelte Liebhaber)
Lieder von Hugo Wolf. Dietrich Fischer-Dieskau. 7-Oden 181 01470/76
1038 Der Gärtner (Mörike) *See also* **1046**
Lieder Recital. Kathleen Ferrier. Rich R 23184
1039 Gesellenlied (Reinick)

WOLF, HUGO—*Continued*
1040 Goethe Lieder (Selections) (Anakreons Grab / Beherzigung I, II / Blumengruss / Cophtisches Lied I, II / Dank des Paria / Epiphanias / Erschaffen und beleben / Fresh and froh I, II / Frühling übers Jahr / Ganymed / Genialisch Treiben / Gleich und gleich / Grenzen der Menschheit / Gutmann und Gutweib / Harfenspieler Lieder / Königlich Gebet / Der neue Amadis / Ob der Koran von Ewigkeit sei? / Phänomen / Prometheus / Der Rattenfänger / Ritter Kurts Brautfahrt / Der Sänger / Sankt Nepomuks Vorabend / Der Schäfer / Sie haben wegen der Trunkenheit / Solang man nüchtern ist / Spottlied / Trunken müssen wir alle sein / Was in der Schenke waren heute)
   Lieder von Hugo Wolf. Dietrich Fischer-Dieskau. 7-Odeon 181 01470/76
1041 Harfenspieler Lieder (Goethe) (Wer sich der Einsamkeit ergibt / An die Türen will ich schleichen / Wer nie sein Brot mit Tränen ass) *See also* 1040
   Schumann and Wolf Lieder. Harold Enns. Orion 74146
1042 Keine gleicht von allen Schönen (Byron)
1043 Der König bei der Krönung (Mörike)
1044 Lied des transferierten Zettel (Shakespeare)
1045 Morgenstimmung (Reinick)
1046 Mörike Lieder (Selections) (Abschied / An den Schlaf / An die Geliebte / Auf ein altes Bild / Auf eine Christblume I, II / Auf einer Wanderung / Auftrag / Begegnung / Bei einer Trauung / Denk es, o Seele / Der Feuerreiter / Fussreise / Der Gärtner / Gebet / Die Geister am Mummelsee / Der Genesene an die Hoffnung / Gesang Weylas / Heimweh / Im Frühling / In der Frühe / Der Jäger / Jägerlied / Karwoche / Lebe wohl / Lied eines Verliebten / Neue Liebe / Nimmersatte Liebe / Peregrina I, II / Schlafendes Jesuskind / Selbstgeständnis / Seufzer / Storchenbotschaft / Der Tambour / Um Mitternacht / Verborgenheit / Wo find ich Trost? / Zitronenfalter im April / Zur Warnung)
   Lieder von Hugo Wolf. Dietrich Fischer-Dieskau. 7-Odeon 181 01470/76
1047 Schlafendes Jesuskind (Mörike) *See also* 1046
   Cornelius and Wolf. Hermann Prey. DG 2530108
1048 Schon streckt ich aus im Bett (Italienisches Liederbuch)
   Heldentenor of the Century. Lauritz Melchior. 3-RCA CRM-3-0308
1049 Sonne der Schlummerlosen (Byron)
   Lieder von Hugo Wolf. Dietrich Fischer-Dieskau. 7-Odeon 181 01470/76
1050 Spanisches Liederbuch (Selections) (Ach des Knaben Augen / Alle gingen, Herz, zur Ruh / Bedeckt mich mit Blumen / Die ihr schwebet um diese Palmen / Führ mich, Kind, nach Bethlehem / Geh', Geliebter, geh' jetzt / Herr, was trägt der Boden hier / In dem Schatten meiner Locken / Köpfchen, Köpfchen, nicht gewimmert / Mögen alle bösen Zungen / Mühvoll komm' ich und beladen / Sagt, seid Ihr es, feiner Herr / Sie blasen zum Abmarsch / Tief im Herzen trag' ich Pein / Trau' nicht der Liebe / Wunden trägst du, mein Geliebter)
   Songs from the Spanisches Liederbuch. Jan De Gaetani. None H 71296
1051 Spanisches Liederbuch (Selections) (Ach, des Knaben Augen / Ach, im Maien war's / Ach wie lang die Seele schlummert / Alle gingen, Herz, zur Ruh / Auf dem grünen Balkon / Blindes Schauen / Da nur Leid und Leidenschaft / Deine Mutter, süsses Kind / Dereinst, dereinst, Gedanke mein / Die du Gott gebarst / Führ mich, Kind / Herr, was trägt der Boden hier / Herz, verzage nicht geschwind / Ich fuhr über Meer / Komm, o Tod / Nun bin ich dein / Nun wandre Maria / Seltsam ist Juanas Weise / Tief im Herzen trag' ich Pein / Treibe nur mit Lieben Spott / Und schläfst du, mein Mädchen / Wenn du zu den Blumen gehst / Wer sein holdes Lieb verloren)
   Lieder von Hugo Wolf. Dietrich Fischer-Dieskau. 7-Odeon 181 01470/76
1052 Ein Ständchen Euch zu bringen (Italienisches Liederbuch)
   Heldentenor of the Century. Lauritz Melchior. 3-RCA CRM-3-0308
1053 Über Nacht (Sturm)
   Lieder von Hugo Wolf. Dietrich Fischer-Dieskau. 7-Odeon 181 01470/76

1054   Verborgenheit (Mörike) *See also* **1046**
        Lieder Recital. Kathleen Ferrier. Rich R 23184
1055   Wanderers Nachtlied (Goethe)
1056   Wo wird einst (Heine)
1057   Zur Ruh', zur Ruh' (Kerner)
        Lieder von Hugo Wolf. Dietrich Fischer-Dieskau. 7-Odeon 181 01470/76

WOODFORDE-FINDEN, AMY (d.1919)
1058   Kashmiri song
        Ballads and Songs of Love and Sentiment. Stuart Burrows. Oiseau SOL 324

WORTH, AMY
1059   Midsummer
        Songs My Mother Taught Me. Joan Sutherland. Lon 26367

ZANDONAI, RICCARDO (1883-1944)
1060   L'assiuolo
        Tebaldi in Concert. Renata Tebaldi. Lon 26303

ZELTER, CARL FRIEDRICH (1758-1832)
1061   Gleich und gleich
1062   Rastlose Liebe
1063   Um Mitternacht
1064   Wo geht's Liebchen
        Frühe Goethe-Lieder. Dietrich Fischer-Dieskau. DG Archive 2533149

RECORD ALBUM INDEX
Works of one composer

ALWYN, WILLIAM
Musical Heritage Society 1742. *William Alwyn.*
Divertimento for solo flute / Mirages / Naiades. Benjamin Luxon, bar; Christopher
Hyde-Smith, fl; Marisa Robles, hp.

BACH, CARL PHILIPP EMANUEL
Deutsche Grammaphon Archive 2533058. *Odes, Psalms and Lieder.*
Abendlied / Bitten / Demut / Der Frühling / Die Güte Gottes / Jesus in Gethsemane /
Morgengesang / Passionslied / Prüfung am Abend / 19 Psalm / 130 Psalm / 148 Psalm /
Der Tag des Weltergerichts / Trost der Erlösung / Über die Finsternis kurz vor dem
Tode Jesu / Weinachtslied / Wider den Übermut. Dietrich Fischer-Dieskau, bar;
Jörg Demus, Tangentenflügel.

BARTOK, BELA
Deutsche Grammaphon 2530405. *Bartók.*
Five songs, Op. 15 / Five songs, Op. 16 / Five village scenes. Julia Hamari, m-sop;
Konrad Richter, pf.

BEETHOVEN, LUDWIG VAN
Deutsche Grammaphon 2530262. *Folk Song Arrangements.*
Behold, my love (duet) / Come fill, fill my good fellow / Duncan Gray (trio) /
Elfin fairies (solo and choir) / Faithful Johnnie (duet) / He promis'd me at parting
(duet) / Highland watch (solo and choir) / Highlander's lament (solo and choir) /
Miller of Dee (trio) / Music, love and wine (trio) / Oh, had my fate been join'd at
parting / Oh sweet were the hours / Pulse of an Irishman / Put round the bright wine.
Edith Mathis, sop; Alexander Young, ten; Dietrich Fischer-Dieskau, bar; RIAS
Kammerchor: Günther Arndt; Andreas Röhn, vl; Georg Donderer, vlc; Karl Engel, pf.

BERG, ALBAN
Columbia M-32162. *Berg.*
Seven early songs / Wozzeck (Act III). Heather Harper, sop; BBC Sym. Orch:
Boulez (in songs); Isabel Strauss, sop; Walter Berry, bs; Chor of Paris Nat. Opera;
Orch. of Paris Nat. Opera: Boulez.

BRAHMS, JOHANNES
Angel S 36753. *Brahms.*
Die schöne Magelone. Dietrich Fischer-Dieskau, bar; Sviatoslav Richter, pf.
BASF KHB-21021. *Brahms Songs.*
Ach, Modr, ich well en Ding han / Ach, wende diesen Blick / Am Sonntag Morgen /
Da unten im Tale / Es steht ein' Lind in jenem Tal / Es träumte mir / Feinsliebchen,
du sollst mir nicht barfuss geh'n / In stiller Nacht / Das Mädchen spricht /
Mädchenlied / O kühler Wald / Schwesterlein / Ständchen / Unbewegte, laue Luft /

BRAHMS, JOHANNES — *Continued*

Vergebliches Ständchen / Von ewiger Liebe / Während des Regens / Wenn du nur zuweilen Lächelst. Elly Ameling, sop; Norman Shetler, pf.

Musical Heritage Society MHS 1377. *Brahms.*

Die schöne Magelone. Bernard Kruysen, bar; Noel Lee, pf.

Richmond R-23183. *Brahms Recital.*

Alto Rhapsody / Botschaft / Geistliches Wiegenlied / Gestille Sehnsucht / Sapphische Ode / Vier ernste Gesänge. Kathleen Ferrier, con; John Newmark, pf; Phyllis Spurr, pf; Max Gilbert, vla; London Phil. Orch: Clemens Krauss.

CRUMB, GEORGE

Columbia M 32739. *Crumb.*

Night of the four moons / Voice of the whale. Jan De Gaetani, m-sop; Aeolian Chamber Players.

DAVIES, PETER MAXWELL

Nonesuch H-71285. *Peter Maxwell Davies.*

Eight songs for a mad king. Julius Eastman, voice; The fires of London: Davies.

DEBUSSY, CLAUDE

Telefunken 22540. *Debussy Songs.*

Fête galantes II / Nöel des enfants qui n'ont plus de Maisons / Le promenoir des deux amants / Trois ballades de Francois Villon / Trois chansons de France / Trois poèmes de Stéphane Mallarmé. Bernard Kruysen, bar; Noel Lee, pf.

DOWLAND, JOHN

Orion 72102. *Lute Songs and Dances.*

Air (lute) / Awake, sweet love / Can she excuse my wrongs / Come again / Come away, come sweet love / Come, heavy sleep / Go crystal tears / Go from my window / Lady Hammond's Alemaine (lute) / Rest awhile you cruel cares / The round battle Gailliard (lute) / The shoemaker's wife (lute) / Tarleton's Resurrection (lute) / Think'st thou then by thy feigning / Wilt thou, unkind, thus reave me. Hayden Blanchard, ten; Frederick Noad, lt; Ruth Adams, vla de gamba.

Turnabout 34510. *Songs and Dances.*

Awake sweet love / Can she excuse / Come again / Come away, come sweet love / Farewell unkind / Fine knacks for ladies / Fortune my foe / The Frog Gailliard (lute) / Mr. Henry Noel's Gailliard (lute) / Mistress Winter's jump / Mrs. White's thing (lute) / Now o now / Orlando sleepth (lute) / Robin is to the greenwood gone (lute) / Say, love, if ever thou did'st find / Sorrow, sorrow, stay / Stay, time, awhile thy flying / Think'st thou then by thy feigning / Weep you no more, sad fountains / What if I never speed / When Phoebus first did Daphne love / White as lilies was her face. Hugues Cuenod, ten; Joel Cohen, lt; Christiane Jaccottet, virginals.

DVORAK, ANTONIN

SUPRA ST 50898. *Dvorak.*

Biblical songs / I dreamed last night / Songs my mother taught me. Véra Soukuporá, con; Ivan Moravec, pf.

FAURE, GABRIEL

Philips 835286. *Fauré.*

Dans la forêt de Septembre / Eau vivante / Exaucement / La fleur qui va sur l'eau / L'horizon chimérique / Je me poserai sur ton coeur / Madrigal / Mélodies de Venise / Mirages / O mort, poussière d'êtoiles / La rose. Gérard Souzay, bar; Dalton Baldwin, pf.

Telefunken 22546. *Fauré Songs.*

Accompagnement / Arpège / La bonne chanson / Dans la forêt de Septembre /

La fleur qui va sur l'eau / Mirages / Le parfum impérissable. Bernard Kruysen, bar; Noel Lee, pf.

FOSTER, STEPHEN
Nonesuch H-71268. *Songs by Stephen Foster.*
Ah, may the red rose live alway / Beautiful dreamer / Gentle Annie / If you've only got a moustache / I'm nothing but a plain old soldier / Jeanie with the light brown hair / Mr. & Mrs. Brown (duet) / Slumber, my darling / Some folks (duet) / Sweetly she sleeps, my Alice fair / That's what's the matter (duet) / There's a good time coming / Was my brother in the battle? / Wilt thou be gone, love? (duet). Jan De Gaetani, m-sop; Leslie Guinn, bar; Gilbert Kalish, pf and melodeon; Sonya Monosoff, vl; Robert Sheldon, fl and keyed bgl.

FRANZ, ROBERT
EDUCO 4017. *Franz Songs.*
Auf dem Teich / Das ist ein Brausen und Heulen / Drüben geht die Sonne scheiden / Durch den Wald im Mondenscheine / Die Farben Helgolands / Der Fichtenbaum / Ein Friedhof / Frühlingsgedränge / Gewitternacht / Gute Nacht / Die helle Sonne leuchtet / Im Herbst / Im Rhein, im heiligen Strome / Die Lotosblume / Marie / Meeresstille / Romanze / Der Schalk / Sonnenuntergang, schwarze Wolken zieh'n / Trübe wird's, die Wolken jagen / Vergessen / Widmung. Peter Del Grande, bar; Mary Elizabeth Handley, pf.

HANDEL, GEORGE FREDERIC
Argo ZRG 504. *Handel Arias.*
Arm, arm ye brave / The god of battle / Honour and arms / O ruddier than the cherry / Peace crown'd with roses / Pensa a chi geme / Revenge, Timotheus cries / Se un bell'ardire / Si, tra i ceppi / Wide spread his mane. Forbes Robinson, bs; The Academy of St. Martin-in-the-Fields: Neville Marriner; Philip Ledger, hpsch.
2-BASF 21687. *Handel Cantatas.*
Ah, che troppo inegali / Look down, harmonius Saint (Praise of harmony) / Nel dolce dell'oblio (Pensiere notturni di Filii) / Silete Venti. Overture to Joseph. Theo Altmeyer, ten; Elly Ameling, sop; Halina Lukonksa, sop; Hans Martin Linde, rec; Johannes Koch, vla da gamba; Gustav Leonhardt, hpsch; Helmut Hucke, ob; Collegium Aureum: Reonhard Peters; Rolf Reinhardt.
Cambridge CRS 2773. *Handel.*
Lucrezia (cantata) / Three arias from "Tamerlano": Deh lasciatemi il nemico / Padre amato, in me riposa / Se non me vuol amar. Carole Bogard, sop; James Weaver, hpsch; Catharina Meints, clo; Chamber Orch. of Copenhagen: John Moriarty.
Philips 6500523. *Handel.*
Lucrezia (cantata) / Care selve (Atalanta) / Dopo notte (Ariodante) / Dove sei, amato bene (Rodelinda) / O had I Jubal's lyre (Joshua) / Ombra mai fu (Serse) / Where shall I fly (Hercules). Janet Baker, m-sop; English Chamber Orch: Leppard.

HAYDN, FRANZ JOSEPH
EMI Electrola C053-01 436. *Haydn Songs.*
Abschiedslied / Auch die sprödeste der Schönen / Die zu späte Ankunft der Mutter / Fidelity / Gegenliebe / Geistliches Lied / Der Gleichsinn / Kaiserlied / Das Leben ist ein Traum / Lob der Faulheit / Piercing eyes / Recollection / Sailor's song / Eine sehr gewöhnliche Geschichte / She never told her love / The spirit's song / The wanderer / Zufriedenheit. Dietrich Fischer-Dieskau, bar; Gerald Moore, pf.

HOVHANESS, ALAN
Poseidon Society 1005. *Hovhaness.*
Black pool of cat / Dawn at Loana / How I adore thee / Love songs of Hafiz / Lullaby of the lake / Out of the depths / Three odes of Solomon. Ara Berberian, bs; Alan Hovhaness, pf.

HOVHANESS, ALAN—*Continued*
Poseidon Society 1008. *Songs of Hovhaness.*
Ararat / Dulhey, Dulhey / The flute player of the Armenian Mountains / Gantznin Orern / Gurge Dikran. Ara Berberian, bs; Alan Hovhaness, pf.
Poseidon Society 1009. *Hovhaness Songs.*
Distant lake of sighs / From high Armenia Mountain / In early dawn time / Live in the sun / Pagan saint / Two Shakespeare sonnets / Under a Byzantine dome. Ara Berberian, bs; Alan Hovhaness, pf.

IVES, CHARLES
Columbia M4 32504. *Charles Ives: The 100th Anniversary.*
Record 1: The fourth of July / The unanswered question / In Flanders Field / Hymn / The pond / Variations on "America" / The circus band / General Booth enters into heaven. N.Y. Phil: Bernstein; Thomas Stewart, bar; Archie Drake, bs; Alan Mandel, pf; N.Y. String Quartet; Pond. Cham. Orch: Schuller; Gregg Smith Singers; Col. Cham. Orch: Smith.
Record 2: The celestial country / They are there / Majority / An election / Lincoln the Great Commoner. Greg Smith Singers; Col. Cham. Orch; American Sym. Orch: Stokowski.
Record 3: Canon / Down east / Feldeinsamkeit / Incantation / Judges' walk / Luck and work / Mists / Requiem / The new river / No more / Old home day / The one way / Peaks / Pictures / Resolution / A sea dirge / The sea of sleep / September / The side show / Slow march / There is a certain garden / The things our fathers loved / West London / Widmung / Yellow leaves. Helen Boatwright, sop; John Kirkpatrick, pf.
Record 4: Ives plays Ives. Study No. 2 / Concord Sonata (excerpts) / They are there.
Record 5: Charles Ives remembers. Reminiscences of the composer by relatives, friends and associates.

KODALY, ZOLTAN
Hungaroton SLP 11450. *Kodály Orchestral Songs.*
A lōzelitō téls / Imhol nyitva én kebelem / Kádár Kata / Mónár Anna / Siralmas nékem / Sirni, sirni / Várj meg madaram. Győrgy Melis, bar; József Simándy, ten; Márta Szirmay, con; Orch. of the Hungarian Radio and TV: Győrgy Lehel.

LISZT, FRANZ
EDUCO 4019. *Liszt Songs.*
Du bist wie eine Blume / Es rauschen die Winde / Die Fischertochter / Kling', leise, mein Lied / Lasst mich ruhen / Die Lorelei / Mignons Lied / Nimm einen Strahl der Sonne / Die stille Wasserrose / Und sprich / Wieder möcht' ich begegnen. Peter Del Grande, bar; Corbett Jones, pf.

MAHLER, GUSTAV
Columbia KM 30942. *Mahler Songs.*
Ablösung im Sommer / Blicke mir nicht in die Lieder / Ich atmet' einen linden Duft / Ich bin der Welt abhanden gekommt / Nicht Wiedersehen / Scheiden und Meiden / Selbstgefühl / Serenade aus "Don Juan" / Um Mitternacht / Um schlimme Kinder artig zu machen / Zu Strassburg auf der Schanz. Dietrich Fischer-Dieskau, bar; Leonard Bernstein, pf.
London CSA 2228. *Mahler.*
Four songs from Des Knaben Wunderhorn: Das irdische Leben / Rheinlegendchen / Verlor'ne Müh / Wo die Trompeten blasen. Symphony No. 5. Yvonne Minton, m-sop; CSO: Solti.
London OS 26195. *Mahler.*
Four songs from Des Knaben Wunderhorn: Das irdische Leben / Rheinlegendchen /

Verlor'ne Müh / Wo die schönen Trompeten blasen. Lieder eines fahrenden Gesellen. Yvonne Minton, m-sop; CSO: Solti.

MEDTNER, NIKOLAI

EDUCO 4016. *Medtner German Songs.*

Alt Mütterlein / Aus "Claudine von Villa-Bella" / Einsamkeit / Elfenliedchen / Erster Verlust / Ein Fichtenbaum steht einsam / Gefunden / Geistergruss / Geweihter Platz / Gleich und gleich / Lieb Liebchen / Im Walde / Mailied / Meeresstille / Nachtgruss / Praeludium / Selbstbetrug / Wanderers Nachtlied I, II / Winternacht. Peter Del Grande, bar; Pavel Mishakov, pf.

Orion 7157. *Medtner Russian Songs.*

Dawn / Day and night / The echo / Elegy, Op. 28, No. 5 / Elegy, Op. 45, No. 1 / Heave, empty and bleak / Midday / The muse / The rose / Signs / Sleeplessness / Spanish romance / Twilight / Verses written during insomnia / Waves and thoughts. Peter Del Grande, bar; Vladimar Pleshakov, pf.

MESSIAEN, OLIVER

Argo ZRG 699. *Messiaen.*

Chants de terre et de ciel / Poèmes pour Mi. Noelle Barker, sop; Robert Sherlaw Johnson, pf.

MOZART, WOLFGANG AMADEUS

Deutsche Grammaphon 2530319. *Mozart Lieder.*

Abendempfindung / Ah, spiegarti, Oh Dio / Als Luise die Briefe / Die Alte / Des kleinen Friedrichs Geburtstag / Der Frühling / Das Kinderspiel / Die kleine Spinnerin / Un moto di gioia / Oiseau, si tous les ans / Ridente la calma / Sehnsucht nach dem Frühlinge / Sei du mein Trost / Das Veilchen / Die Verschweigung / Der Zauberer / Die Zuffriedenheit. Edith Mathis, sop; Bernhard Klee, pf.

Hungaroton 11485. *Concert Arias.*

Con ossequio, con rispetto K. 210 / Misero, o sogno, o son desto K. 431 / Per pietà non ricercate K 420 / Se al labbro mio non credi K. 295 / Si mostra la sorte K. 209. József Réti, ten; Budapest Phil: Antal Jancsovics.

Philips 6500544. *Mozart Opera and Concert Arias.*

Cosi Fan Tutte: Temerari! sortite guori di questo loco - Come scoglio. Don Giovanni: Batti, batti. Vedrai carino. Idomeneo: Ch'io me scordi di te? Le Nozze Di Figaro: Deh vieni non tardar / Non so più / Voi che sapete. Chi sa, chi sa, qual sia K. 582 / Misera, dove son K. 369 / Vado, me dove? K. 583. Elly Ameling, sop; English Chamber Orch: Edo de Waart.

Supra-1-12-1114. *Mozart Soprano Arias.*

Bella mia fiamma, addio K. 528 / Mia speranza adorata K. 416 / No, no, che non sei capace K. 419 / Popoli di Tessaglia . . . Io non chiedo, eterni Dei K. 300b / Schon lacht der holde Frühling K. 580. Jana Jonásová, sop; Prague Cham. Orch: Lukás.

POULENC, FRANCIS

Turnabout 4489. *Songs of Poulenc.*

Air romantique / Avant le cinéma / Cinq poèmes de Paul Eluard / Le grenouillère / Huit chansons polonaises / Nuage / Le travail du peintre. Rose Dercourt, sop; Francis Poulenc, pf.

RACHMANINOFF, SERGEI

Angel S-36917. *Rachmaninoff Songs.*

The answer / Arion / At my window / Christ is risen / Day and night / The floods of spring / Fragment of Alfred de Musset / The harvest of sorrow / How fair this spot / In the silence of the night / Lilacs / The morn of life / Oh, do not grieve / Oh, never sing to me again / The storm / To the children / Vocalise. Nicolai Gedda, ten; Alexis Weissenberg, pf.

RACHMANINOFF, SERGEI—*Continued*
EDUCO 4018. *Rachmaninoff Songs.*

Although I beg you / April / Spring holiday / Do you have hiccups? / Don't leave me / The flower has wilted / Harvest fields / How long, my friend your sorrowful gaze / I will not tell you / In the silent and mysterious night / Letter to K.S. Stanislavsky from S. Rachmaninoff / Meditation / Night / O, do not sing fair maiden / The song of the disillusioned one. Peter Del Grande, bar; Laurette Goldberg, pf.

Orion 73109. *Song Selections.*

Arion / By my window / Extreme happiness / The fountain / I remember that day / I was with her / Impossible / In my spirit / Lazarus has risen / The muse / Music / Paid in full / The spirit is within us / The tempest / These summer nights / Wind all around / Yesterday we met / You knew him. Peter Del Grande, bar; Vladimar Pleshakov, pf.

RIMSKY-KORSAKOV, NIKOLAI
EDUCO 4020. *Rimsky-Korsakov Songs.*

An angel is flying through the midnight sky / Conjuring / The echo / From my tears my little one, there were born many fragrant flowers / The golden cloud slept / I awaited you in the grotto / In the dark bouquet, the nightingale fell silent / The messenger / The nightingale's infatuation with the rose / The pine tree and the palm / Place your cheek against mine / The secret / Silence descends on the yellow fields / The soul flew softly through the heavens / There, where you are, my thoughts are flying / Upon the hills of Georgia / What good will be my name to you? / When waves the yellowing field of corn / Zuleika's song. Peter Del Grande, bar; Mary Elizabeth Handley, pf.

SCHOENBERG, ARNOLD
2-Columbia M31311/2. *Complete Songs for Voice and Piano.*

Two songs, Op. 1 / Four songs, Op. 2 / Six songs, Op. 3 / Eight songs, Op. 6 / Two ballads, Op. 12 / Two songs, Op. 14 / Das Buch der hängenden Gärten, Op. 15 / Three songs, Op. 48 / Two songs, Op. (Posthumous). Ellen Faull, sop; Helen Vanni, m-sop; Donald Gramm, bs-bar; Cornelis Opthof, bar; Glenn Gould, pf.

SCHUBERT, FRANZ
Deutsche Grammaphon 2530229. *Schubert Lieder to Goethe Texts.*

An den Mond D. 259 / An den Mond D. 296 / Erlkönig / Der Fischer / Gesänge des Harfners I, II, III / Heidenröslein / Meeres Stille / Nachtgesang / Nahe des Geliebten / Rastlose Liebe / Der Sänger / Schäfers Klagelied / Wanderers Nachtlied D. 224. Dietrich Fischer-Dieskau, bar; Gerald Moore, pf.

Deutsche Grammaphon 2530306. *Schiller Lieder.*

An den Frühling / An die Freude / Die Bürgschaft / Das Geheimnis / Die Götter Griechenlands / Gruppe aus dem Tartarus / Der Jüngling am Bache / Das Mädchen aus der Fremde / Der Pilgrim / Sehnsucht. Dietrich Fischer-Dieskau, bar; Gerald Moore, pf.

Deutsche Grammaphon 2530347. *Schubert Lieder.*

Abendstern / Am See / Auflösung / Der blinde Knabe / Grablied / Herrn Joseph Spaun / Im Haine / Der Jüngling auf dem Hügel / Der Jüngling und der Tod / Der Knabe in der Wiege / Leiden der Trennung / Der Strom / Totengrabers Heimweh / Der Vater mit dem Kind / Wehmut / Der zürnende Barde / Der Zwerg. Dietrich Fischer-Dieskau, bar; Gerald Moore, pf.

Deutsche Grammaphon 2530404. *Schubert Lieder.*

Am Bach im Frühling / An die Nachtigall / Auf der Donau / Ave Maria / Des Mädchens Klage / Frühlingsglaube / Gretchen am Spinnrade / Im Abendrot / Die junge Nonne / Der König in Thule / Lachen und Weinen / Mignon's song / Romanze / Die Rose / Der Tod und das Mädchen. Christa Ludwig, m-sop; Irwin Cage, pf.

4-Deutsche Grammophon 2720059. *Volume III.*
Die schöne Müllerin / Schwanengesang / Die Winterreise. Dietrich Fischer-Dieskau, bar; Gerald Moore, pf.
London 26251.
Die schöne Müllerin. Herman Prey, bar; Karl Engel, pf.
London OS 26328.
Schwanengesang. Tom Krause, bar; Irwin Cage, pf.
Philips 650015. *Goethe Songs.*
Heidenröslein / Die Liebende schreibt / Liebhaber in allen Gestalten / Lied der Mignon I, II, III, IV / Nähe des Geliebten. Elly Ameling, sop; Dalton Baldwin, pf. Erlkönig / Ganymed / Gesänge des Harfners / Der Sänger. Herman Prey, bar; Karl Engel, pf.
Philips 6747033.
Die Winterreise. Hermann Prey, bar; Wolfgang Sawallisch, pf.
2-Seraphim S-6083. *Janet Baker Sings Schubert.*
An die Nachtigall / An die untergehende Sonne / Ave Maria / Berthas Lied in der Nacht / Delphine / Des Mädchens Klage / Herrn Josef von Spaun / Gretchen am Spinnrade / Heiss mich nicht reden / Hin und wieder / Iphigenia / Jäger, ruhe von der Jagd / Die junge Nonne / Kennst du das Land / Liebe schwärmt / Die Männer sind méchant / Nur wer die Sehnsucht kennt / Raste, Krieger / Schlummerlied / Schwestergruss / So lasst mich scheinen / Suleika I, II / Wiegenlied D. 498 / Wiegenlied D. 867. Janet Baker, m-sop; Gerald Moore, pf.

SCHUMANN, ROBERT
Argo ZRD 718. *Schumann.*
Liederkreis, Op. 24 / Liederkreis, Op. 39. Robert Tear, ten; Philip Ledger, pf.
BASF 26369. *Lieder.*
Aufträge / Er ist's / Erstes Grün / Frage / Jasminenstrauch / Die Kartenlegerin / Das Käuzlein / Die letzten Blumen starben / Loreley / Marienwürmchen / Die Meerfee / Mein schönen Stern / Der Sandman / Sehnsucht / Sehnsucht nach der Waldgegend / Die Sennin / Schmetterling / Schneeglöckchen / Waldesgespräch / Widmung. Elly Ameling, sop; Jörg Demus, pf.
Odeon 163-11325. *Schumann.*
Ihre Stimme / Kerner Lieder / Mein schöner Stern / Nachtlied / Schneeglöckchen / Widmung / Zwei Venetianische Lieder. Gérard Souzay, bar; Dalton Baldwin, pf.
6-Valois CMB 17. *Les Lieder de 1840.*
Belsatzar / Dichterliebe / Five Lieder, Op. 40 / Frauenliebe und Leben / Gedichte, Op. 30 / Gedichte, Op. 35 / Gedichte, Op. 36 / Gesänge, Op. 31 / Lieder und Gesänge, Op. 27 / Lieder und Gesänge, Op. 51 / Liebesfrühling, Op. 37 / Liederkreis, Op. 24 / Liederkreis, Op. 39 / Myrthen, Op. 25 / Romanzen und Balladen I, Op. 45 / Romanzen und Balladen II, Op. 49 / Romanzen und Balladen III, Op. 53. Danielle Galland, sop; Bernard Kruysen, bar; Noel Lee, pf.

TCHAIKOVSKY, PETER ILYITCH
Argo ZRG 707. *Tchaikovsky Songs.*
Again, as before / As over hot embers / Cradle song / Disappointment / Do not believe me, my dear / Do not leave me / Don Juan's serenade / Great deeds / In the clamour of the ballroom / Mignon's song / My genius, my angel, my friend: Reconcilement / My little minx / No answer, no word, no greeting / O stay / They kept on saying "you fool" / Through the window / To forget so soon, is it not so? Robert Tear, ten; Philip Ledger, pf.
Orion 74156. *Tchaikovsky Songs.*
At the ball / Darkness has fallen / Day is reigning / A dead man's love / Don Juan's serenade / Evening / Fearful moment / Florentine song / I bless you forests /

TCHAIKOVSKY, PETER ILYITCH – *Continued*
Look, yonder floats / Neither an answer / No, I will never name / O, if you only could / That was in early springtime. Peter Del Grande, bar; Vladimir Pleshakov, pf.

VAUGHAN WILLIAMS, RALPH
Argo ZRG 732. *Songs by Vaughan Williams.*
Linden Lea / Orpheus with his lute / Songs of travel / Ten Blake songs for voice and oboe. Robert Tear, ten; Philip Ledger, pf; Neil Black, oboe.

WEIGL, KARL
Turnabout 34522. *Karl Weigl Songs.*
Abendstunde (duet) / Beatrix / Blaue Nacht / Ehestand der Freude (duet) / Es goss mein volles Leben / Five Lieder aus "Phantasus" / Halleluja der Sonne / Hymne (duet) / In goldenen Fülle (duet) / Liebeslied / Lied der Schiffermädels / Lieder der Liebe und Einsamkeit / O Nacht, du silberbleiche / Schlummerlied / Seele / Spielmannslied / Das unsichtbare Licht / Der Wanderer und das Blumenmädchen (duet) / Wiegenlied. Betty Allen, m-sop; Colette Boky, sop; Judith Raskin, sop; George Shirley, ten; William Warfield, bar; David Garvey, pf.

WOLF, HUGO
Nonesuch H-71296. *Songs from the Spanisches Liederbuch.*
Ach, des Knaben Augen / Alle gingen, Herz, zur Ruh / Bedeckt mich mit Blumen / Die ihr schwebet / Führ' mich, Kind, nach Bethlehem / Geh', Geliebter, geh' jetzt / Herr, was trägt der Boden hier / In den Schatten meiner Locken / Köpfchen, Köpfchen, nicht gewimmert / Mögen alle bösen Zungen / Mühvoll komm' ich und beladen / Sagt, seid Ihr es, feiner Herr / Sie blasen zum Abmarsch / Tief im Herzen trag' ich Pein / Trau' nicht der Liebe / Wunden trägst du, mein Geliebter. Jan De Gaetani, m-sop; Gilbert Kalish, pf.
Odeon 181 01470-76. *Lieder von Hugo Wolf.*
Eichendorff Lieder (Selections): Erwartung / Der Freund / Der Glücksritter / Heimweh / In der Fremde I / Lieber alles / Liebesglück / Der Musikant / Nachruf / Die Nacht / Nachtzauber / Der Scholar / Der Schreckenberger / Seemanns Abschied / Der Soldat I, II / Das Ständchen Unfall / Verschwiegene Liebe / Der verzweifelte Liebhaber. Goethe Lieder (Selections): Anakreons Grab / Beherzigung I, II / Blumengruss / Cophtisches Lied I, II / Dank des Paria / Epiphanias / Erschaffen und beleben / Fresh und froh I, II / Frühling übers Jahr / Ganymed / Genialisch Treiben / Gleich und gleich / Grenzen der Menschheit / Gutmann und Gutweib / Harfenspieler Lieder / Königlich Gebet / Der neue Amadis / Ob der Koran von Ewigkeit sei / Phänomen / Prometheus / Der Rattenfänger / Ritter Kurts Braufahrt / Der Sänger / Sankt Nepomuks Vorabend / Der Schäfer / Sie haben wegen der Trunkenheit / Solang man nüchtern ist / Spottlied / Trunken müssen wir alle sein / Was in der Schenke waren heute. Mörike Lieder (Selections): Abschied / An den Schlaf / An die Geliebte / Auf ein altes Bild / Auf eine Christblume I, II / Auf einer Wanderung / Auftrag / Begegnung / Bei einer Trauung / Denk es, o Seele / Der Feuerreiter / Fussreise / Der Gärtner / Gebet / Die Geister am Mummelsee / Der Genesene an die Hoffnung / Gesang Weylas / Heimweh / Im Frühling / In der Frühe / Der Jäger / Jägerlied / Karwoche / Lebe wohl / Lied eines Verliebten / Nimmersatte Liebe / Peregrina I, II / Schlafendes Jesuskind / Selbstgeständnis / Seufzer / Storchenbotschaft / Der Tambour / Um Mitternacht / Verborgenheit / Wo find ich Trost? / Zitronenfalter im April / Zur Warnung. Spanisches Liederbuch (Selections): Ach, des Knaben Augen / Ach, im Maien war's / Lied des transferierten Zettel / Morgenstimmung / Sonne der Schlummerlosen / Über Nacht / Wanderers Nachtlied / Wo wird einst / Zur Ruh' zur Ruh'. Dietrich Fischer-Dieskau, bar; Gerald Moore, pf.

RECORD ALBUM INDEX
Works of two or more composers, by manufacturer

ABC

ATS-20011. *Beverly Sills Concert.*
  ADAM: Variations on a theme of Mozart - Bravour: Ah, vous dirai-je, maman
  ARNE: The soldier tir'd
  BISHOP: Lo, here the gentle lark
  CALDARA: Cantata "La Rosa"
  HANDEL: Meine Seele hört im Sehen
  SCHUBERT: Der Hirt auf dem Felsen
Beverly Sills, sop; The Chamber Music Society of Lincoln Center

ANGEL

S-36896. *The Concert at Hunter College.*
  FALLA: Siete canciones populares espanolas
  GIMENEZ: Zapateado
  GRANADOS: Amor y odio / Callajeo / Gracia mia / Iban al pinar / Llorad, corazón /
    La maja de Goya / El majo discreto / El majo olvidado / El majo timido /
    Mananica era / Mira que soy nina / Il mirar de la maja / No lloreis, o juilos / Las
    surrutacas modestas / El tra la la y el punteado
  LASERNA (Arr. Roma): El Tripili
  LITERES (Arr. Tarragó): Confiado jilguerille (Acis y Galatea)
Victoria de los Angeles, sop; Alicia de Larrocha, pf.

S-36897. *Canteloube and Chausson.*
  CANTELOUBE: Songs of the Auvergne
  CHAUSSON: Poème de l'amour et de la mer
Victoria de los Angeles, sop; Lamoureux Concerts Orch: Jacquillat

S-36904. *Baroque—Sacred and Profane*
  BACH: Ächzen und erbärmlich Weinen (Cantata No. 13) / Lass', o Welt
    (Cantata No. 123)
  HANDEL: Cora sposa (Rinaldo)
  RAMEAU: Thétis
  TELEMANN: Ihr Völker, hört
Dietrich Fischer-Dieskau, bar; Robert Veyron-Lacroix, hpsch; Jean-Pierre Rampal, fl;
Jacques Neilz, vlc.

ARGO

ZRG 661. *Robert Tear sings Handel, Arne, Boyce, Hook.*
  ARNE: Bacchus and Ariadne / Fair Caelia love pretended
  BOYCE: Momus to Mars
  HANDEL: Look down, harmonius saint / Meine Seele hört in Sehen / Süsse Stille

ZRG 661 — *Continued*
    HOOK: The lass of Richmond Hill
Robert Tear, ten; Academy of St. Martin-in-the-Fields: Marriner; Simon Preston, hpsch; Iona Brown, vl; Kenneth Heath, clo.

ZRG 664. *Recital.*
    BEETHOVEN: An die ferne Geliebte / Bitten / Busslied / Die ehre Gottes aus der Natur / Gottes Macht und Vorsehung / Die Liebe des Nächsten / Vom Tode
    BRAHMS: Kein Haus, kein Heimat / Mein Herz ist schwer / Mit vierzig Jahren / Sapphische Ode / Steig auf, geliebter Schatten / Vier ernste Gesänge
John Shirley-Quirk, bar; Martin Isepp, pf.

ZRG 703. *Messiaen and Tippett.*
    MESSIAEN: Poèmes pour Mi
    TIPPETT: Songs for Dov
Felicity Palmer, sop; Robert Tear, ten; BBC Sym. Orch: Boulez; London Sinfonietta: Atherton

BASF

20799. *Recital.*
    DEBUSSY: Apparition / Clair de lune (1844) / Fêtes galantes I / Fleur des blés / Pierrot / Rondel chinois
    STRAUSS: All mein Gedanken / Als mir dein Lied erklang / Amor / Ich schwebe / Morgen / Säusle, liebe Myrte / Ständchen
Roberta Peters, sop.

BRUNO WALTER SOCIETY

707. *Song Recital.*
    BRAHMS: Botschaft / Immer leiser wird mein Schlummer / Der Tod das ist die kühle Nacht / Von ewiger Liebe
    SCHUBERT: Du bist die Ruh / Du liebst mich nicht / Die junge Nonne / Romanze aus Rosamunde / Der Tod und das Mädchen
    SCHUMANN: Frauenliebe und Leben
Kathleen Ferrier, con; Bruno Walter, pf.

SID 722. *German Lieder.*
    BRAHMS: An eine Aeolsharfe / Bitteres zu sagen / Blinde Kuh / Es träumte mir / Der Jäger / Nichtigall / Vergebliches Ständchen / Wiegenlied
    SCHUMANN: Er ist's / Frauenliebe und Leben / Mondnacht / Der Nussbaum / O ihr Herren / Röselein / Schneeglockchen / Ständchen
Elisabeth Schumann, sop; Instrumental Accompaniment

CAMBRIDGE

CRS 2715. *Favorite American Concert Songs.*
    BARBER: The daisies / I hear an army / Monks and raisins / Nocturne / Rain has fallen / Sleep now / Sure on this shining night / With Rue my heart is laden
    CHARLES: My lady walks in loveliness
    DUKE: Luke Havergal
    GRIFFES: The lament of Ian the Proud
    HAGEMAN: Do not go, my love
    HOMER: The sick rose
    ROGERS: The time for making songs has come
    SPEAKS: On the road to Mandalay
Dale Moore, bar; Betty Ruth Tomdohrde, pf.

CANTILENA

6237. *Songs.*
Arias **DELIBES:** Lakmé, ton doux regard (Lakmé)
    ELGAR: O my warriors (Caractacus)
    MASSENET: Touraine est un pays (Panurge)
    MOZART: Deh vieni alla finestra (Don Giovanni)
    PALADILHE: Pauvre martyr obscur (Patrie)
    THOMAS: Ombre chere (Hamlet)
    VERDI: Alla vita (Ballo in Maschera) / Di provenza il mar (La Traviata) / Felice ancor (Don Carlo)
Songs **BRAHMS:** Sonntag
    BRIDGE: Go not happy day
    HAHN: A Chloris
    HOMER: Requiem
    LOEWE: Tom der Reimer
    QUILTER: It was a lover and his lass
    SCARLATTI: Gia il sole dal Gange
    SIBELIUS: Svarta Roser
    STRAUSS: Zueignung
    TRAD: The harp that once through Tara's halls
John Stratton, bar; Avey Byram, pf.

CORONET

2818. *Italian Chamber Music.*
    BELLINI: L'allegro marinaro / Quando incise su quel marmo / Vaga luna che inargenti
    CALDARA: Sebben crudele
    CARISSIMI: Vittoria, vittoria
    DURANTE: Vergin tutt'amor
    GASPARINI: Lasciar d'amarti
    ROSA: Vado ben spesso cangiando loco
    ROSSINI: L'ultimo ricordo
    SCARLATTI: Sento nel core
    SPONTINI: Bien peu de chose / Il faut helas
    STRADELLA: Pietà signore
    TORELLI: Tu lo sai
    VERDI: Brindisi
Dicran Jamgochian, bar; Michael Phelps, pf.

CRI

SD 270. *Elwell, Verrall, Walker.*
    ELWELL: A child's grace / I look back / The ouselcock / Service of all the dead / This glittering grief / Wistful
    VERRALL: String Quartet No. 7
    WALKER: Spatials / Piano Sonata No 2 / Spektra
Maxine Makas, sop; Anthony Makas, pf; The Berkshire Quartet; George Walker, pf.

SD 294. *Del Tredici and Diamond.*
    DEL TREDICI: I hear an army / Scherzo
    DIAMOND: Nonet
Phyllis Bryn-Julson, sop; Composers Quartet; Robert Helps, pf; David Del Tredici, pf; String Ensemble: Wuorinen

CRI—*Continued*
  SD 301. *Rhodes, Smith, Ronsheim, Mamlok.*
    MAMLOK: Stray birds
    RHODES: Autumn setting
    RONSHEIM: Bitter-sweet / Easter-wings
    SMITH: Envoy in autumn / Spring / The valley wind / Velvet shoes
  Jan De Gaetani, m-sop; Phyllis Bryn-Julson, sop; Hilda Harris, sop; Zita Carno, pf;
  Raymond Des Roches, vbrph; Harvey Sollberger, fl; Fred Sherry clo; Speculum Musicae

DESTO

  DC 7118-9. *Jennie Tourel at Alice Tully Hall.*
    BEETHOVEN: An die Hoffnung, Op. 94 / Ich liebe dich
    BERLIOZ: L'absence
    DARGOMIJSKY: Romance
    DEBUSSY: Chansons de Bilitis
    GLINKA: Doubt / Vain temptation
    HAHN: Si mes vers avaient des ailes
    LISZT: "Comment" disaient-ils / Mignons Lied / O, quand je dors / Über allen
      Gipfeln ist Ruh' / Vergiftet sind meine Lieder
    MASSANET: Elegy
    MONSIGNY: La sagesse est un trésor
    OFFENBACH: Le barbe bleu / Laughing song (La Périchole)
    STRADELLA: Per pietà
    TCHAIKOVSKY: None but the lonely heart
  Jennie Tourel, m-sop; James Levine, pf; Gary Karr, bs

DEUTSCHE GRAMMOPHON

  2530107. *Songs of the New Vienna School.*
    BERG: Nun ich der Riesen stärksten überwand / Schlafend trägt man mich /
      Schlafen, schlafen / Warme die Lüfte
    SCHOENBERG: Die Aufgeregten / Erwartung / Geübtes Herz / Ich darf nicht
      danken / Sommermüd / Tot / Verlassen
    WEBERN: Am Ufer / An baches ranft / Bild der Liebe / Dies ist ein lied Gefunden /
      Ihr tratet zu dem herde / Noch zwingt mich treue / So ich traurig bin / Vorfrühling
  Dietrich Fischer-Dieskau, bar; Aribert Reimann, pf.

  2530108. *Cornelius and Wolf.*
    CORNELIUS: Vaterunser / Weinachtslieder
    WOLF: Auf ein altes Bild / Schlafendes Jesuskind
  Hermann Prey, bar; Leonard Hokanson, pf

  2530332. *Sonnets of Petrarch.*
    LISZT: Benedetto sia'l giorno / L'vidi in terra angelici costumi / Pace non trovo
    PFITZNER: Voll jener süsse
    REICHARD: Canzon, s'al dolce loco / Di tempo in tempo / Erano i capei d'oro /
      O poggi, o valli, o fiumi / Or ch'il ciel / Più volte già dal bel sembiante
    SCHUBERT: Allein, nachdenklich, gelähmt / Apollo, lebet noch dein hold
      Verlangen / Nunmehr, da Himmel, Erde schweigt
  Dietrich Fischer-Dieskau, bar; Gerald Moore, pf.

DG ARCHIVE

  2533123. *Das Wiener Lied um Schubert.*
    KANNE: Des Alten Abschied / Die Träume
    KREUTZER: Frühlingsglaube / Wehmut
    KRUFFT: An Emma

TEYBER: Liebesschmerz
TOMASCHEK: Abendlied / An den Mond / An Linna / Rastlose Liebe / Schäfers
Klaglied / Selbstbetrug / Trost in Tränen / Wanderers Nachtlied
Hermann Prey, bar; Leonard Hokanson, pf.

2533149. *Frühe Goethe-Lieder.*
ARNIM: O schaudre nicht
BEETHOVEN: Mit Mädeln sich vertragen
HUMMEL: Zur Logenfeier
KREUTZER: Ein Bettler vor dem Tor
NEEFE: Serenate
REICHARDT: An Lotte / Einschränkung / Einziger Augenblick / Feiger Gedanken /
Gott / Mut / Rhapsodie / Die schöne Nacht / Tiefer liegt die Nacht um mich her
SACHSEN-WEIMAR: Auf dem Land und in der Stadt / Sie scheinen zu spielen
SECKENDORFF: Romanze
WAGNER: Branders Lied / Lied des Mephistopheles
ZELTER: Rastlose Liebe / Um Mitternacht / Wo geht's Liebchen? / Gleich
und gleich
Dietrich Fischer-Dieskau, bar; Jörg Demus, pf.

DIS

3700. *Schumann and Wagner.*
SCHUMANN: Frauenliebe und Leben
WAGNER: Wesendonck Lieder
Kathleen Ferrier, con; Kirsten Flagstad, sop; Bruno Walter, pf.

DUKE

DWR 7306. *The Art Song in America, Volume 2.*
CUMMING: Go, lovely rose / The little black boy / Memory / Hither come
DUKE: I carry your heart / in just spring / the mountains are dancing
EARLS: Entreat me not to leave you / Love seeketh not itself to please
PERSICHETTI: The death of a soldier / The grass / Of the surface of things / The
snow man / Thou child so wise
ROREM: A Christmas carol / Clouds / For Susan / Guilt / What sparks and
wiry cries
TRIMBLE: Love seeketh not itself to please / Tell me where is fancy bred?
John Hanks, ten; Ruth Friedberg-Erickson, pf.

KLAVIER

KS 513. *Album of Ayres.*
ANON: Trista sort'e la mia sorte / Belle qui m'avez
ATTAIGNANT: Au joly bois
BOSSINENSUS: Haime per che m'ai privo
DOWLAND: Flow my tears
FORD: Since first I saw your face
HOFHAIMER: Hertzliebstes Pild
MORLEY: O mistress mine
MUDARRA: Claro y Frescos Rios si uiesse e me leuasse
SENFL: Ach Elselein liebes Elselein mein / Die Weyber mit den flohen
SERMISY: Secourses moy, tant que vivray
SHAKESPEARE: How should I your true love know / When that I was a little
tiny boy
TROMBONCINO: Poi che volse la mia stella
Donna Curry, sop and lute

LONDON

STS 15164. *Romantic Songs.*
 BELLINI: L'abandono / Almen se non poss'io / Bella Nice / Il fervido desiderio / Malinconia, ninfa gentile / Per pietà, bell'idol mio
 DONIZETTI: A mezzanotte / Amore e morte / Eterno amore e fè / Meine Liebe / Me voglio f'na casa
 ROSSINI: La gita in gondola / L'orgia / La partenza / La serenata (duet)
Lydia Marimpietri, sop; Ugo Benelli, ten; Enrico Fabbro, pf.

OS 26141. *Britten and Tchaikovsky.*
 BRITTEN: The poet's echo
 TCHAIKOVSKY: At the ball / Night / On the golden cornfield / Serenade / Why, why did I dream of you?
Galina Vishnevskaya, sop; Rostropovich, pf.

26240. *A Lieder Recital.*
 KILPENIN: Jänka / Kesäyö / Kirkkorannassa / Laululle / Rannalta I / Suvilaulu / Tunturille / Vanha kirkko
 SCHUMANN: Kerner Lieder, Op. 35
Martti Talvela, bs; Irwin Gage, pf.

OS 26249. *Russian Songs.*
 BORODIN: For the shores of thy fair native land
 DARGOMIZHSKY: The old corporal / A pleasant nocturnal breeze / The worm
 GLINKA: The midnight review
 RUBINSTEIN: Melody
 TCHAIKOVSKY: Don Juan's serenade / I bless you forests / It was in the early spring / Mid the din of the ball / None but the weary heart / Not a word, o my friend
Nicolai Ghiaurov, bs; Zietina Ghiaurov, pf.

OS 26301. French and Spanish Songs.
 BIZET: Absence / Adieux de l'hotesse arabe / Chanson d'avril / Vieille chanson
 DEBUSSY: Chansons de Bilitis
 FALLA: Seven popular songs
 NIN: Jesus de Nazareth / Villancico andaluz / Villancico asturiano / Villancico castellano
Marilyn Horne, m-sop; Martin Katz, pf.

26303. *Tebaldi in Concert.*
 BELLINI: Malinconia ninfa gentile
 CIMARA: Stornello
 DONIZETTI: Me voglio f'na casa
 GLUCK: O del mio dolce ardor
 MERCADANTE: La sposa del marinaro
 MASCAGNI: La tua stella / Serenata
 PARADISI: M'he presa alla sua ragna
 PERGOLESI: Se tu m'ami
 PONCHIELLI: Non leggevamo insieme
 PUCCINI: E l'uccelino
 RICCI: Il carretiere del Vomero
 ROSSINI: L'invito-bolero
 SCARLATTI: O cessate di piagarmi
 TOSTI: Sogno
 ZANDONAI: L'assiuolo
Renata Tebaldi, sop; Richard Bonynge, pf.

26367. Songs My Mother Taught Me.
 ABT: Der Kukuck

DELIBES: Les filles de Cadiz / Le rossignol
DEL RIEGO: Homing
DVORAK: Songs my mother taught me
GOUNOD: Sérénade
GRIEG: Solvejg's song
HAHN: Si mes vers avaient des ailes
JUNCKER: I was dreaming
LA FORGE: I came with a song
LISZT: Oh, quand je dors
MASSENET: Crépuscule / Oh, si les fleurs avaient des yeux
MENDELSSOHN: Auf Flügeln des Gesanges
NELSON: Mary of Argyll
WORTH: Midsummer
Joan Sutherland, sop; New Phil. Orch: Bonynge

MELODIYA/ANGEL

SR 40198. *Songs.*
    MUSSORSKY: Songs and dances of death
    RACHMANINOFF: Child, thou art fair as a flower/ A dream / Fragment of Alfred
    de Musset / In the silent night / I wait for thee / Lilacs / O cease thy singing,
    maiden fair
Irina Arkhipova, m-sop; John Wustman, pf.

ODYSSEY

Y 32675. *Song Recital.*
    MAHLER: Blicke mir nicht in die Lieder / Ich atmet' einen linden Duft / Ich bin
    der Welt abhanden gekommen
    MARX: Hat dich die Liebe berührt / Valse de Chopin
    STRAUSS: Four last songs / Die Nacht / Cäcilie
Ljuba Welitsch, sop; Paul Ulanowsky, pf.

Y2 32880. *A Tribute to Jennie Tourel.*
    BELLINI: Sgombra è la sacra delva (Norma)
    BIZET: Adieu de l'hôtesse arabe / Carmen: Card song / Gypsy song / Habanera /
    Seguidilla
    CHOPIN: Niema Czego Trzeba / Zyczenie
    DEBUSSY: Chansons de Bilitis
    GINASTERA: Triste
    MUSSORGSKY: Songs and dances of death
    NIN: Pano Murciano
    OBRADORS: Coplas de Curro Dulce
    RAVEL: Chansons Madécasses / Vocalise
    ROSSINI: Bel raggio lusinghier (Semiramide) / Cruda sorte (L'Italiana in Algeri) /
    Non piè mèsta (Cenerentola) / Una voce poco fa (Il Barbiere di Siviglia)
    SATIE: Le chapelier / Je te veux
    VILLA-LOBOS: Cancao do Carriero
Jennie Tourel, m-sop; George Reeves, pf; Leonard Bernstein, pf; Met. Opera Orch:
Cimara, Cleva; Col. Sym. Orch: Morel; Orch: Villa-Lobos; John Wummer, fl;
Laszlo Vargo, clo.

OISEAU

142. *Songs for Courtiers and Cavaliers.*
    CACCINI: Dolcissimo sospiro
    CALESTANI: Damigella tutta bella / Folgorate
    CIFRA: In quel gelato core

142 — *Continued*
　　D'INDIA: Torna il sereno zeffiro / Infelice Didone
　　GRANDI: Vientene o mi crudel
　　LAWES: Among rosebuds / A complaint against Cupid / Disuasion from presumption /
　　　　An eccho / Hymn to God the Father / Hymn to God the Holy Ghost / Hymn to
　　　　God the Son / I prithee send me back my heart / A lady to a young courtier / No
　　　　constancy in man / Parting / Sufferance / Tavola - In quel gelato core
Helen Watts, con; Thurston Dart, hpsch.

SOL 323. *Recital.*
　　FAURE: Lydia / Nell / Prison / Sylvie / Toujours
　　HANDEL: Waft her angels (Jephtha)
　　QUILTER: To Julia
　　SCARLATTI: Sento nel core / Son tutta duolo / Le violette
　　SCHUBERT: Du bist die Ruh' / Heidenröslein / Der Neugierige
Stuart Burrows, ten; John Constable, pf.

SOL 324. *Ballads and Songs of Love and Sentiment.*
　　ADAMS: Nirvana
　　BOHM: Still as the night
　　BOND: A perfect day
　　BOUGHTON: Faery song
　　CADMAN: At dawning
　　CAPEL: Love, could I only tell thee
　　CLAY: I'll sing thee songs of Araby
　　COLERIDGE-TAYLOR: Eleanore
　　GLOVER: The rose of Tralee
　　LESLIE: Annabelle Lee
　　METCALF: Absent
　　MUNRO: My lovely Celia
　　NELSON: Mary of Argyle
　　NEVIN: The rosary
　　SANDERSON: Until
　　SULLIVAN: The lost chord
　　TOSELLI: Serenata
　　TOSTI: My dreams
　　WILLIAMS: My little Welsh home
　　WOODFORDE-FINDEN: Kashmiri song
Stuart Burrows, ten; John Constable, pf.

S-327. *Mahler and Schumann.*
　　MAHLER: Lieder und Gesänge aus der Jugendzeit
　　SCHUMANN: Liederkreis, Op. 39
Anna Reynolds, m-sop; Geoffrey Parsons, pf.

COL-331. *Maconchy and Walton*
　　MACONCHY: Ariadne
　　WALTON: Three songs: Daphne / Through gilded trellises / Old Sir Faulk /
　　　　A song for the Lord Mayor's table (cycle)
Heather Harper, sop; Paul Hamburger, pf; English Cham. Orch: Leppard

ORION

74146. *Schumann and Wolf Lieder.*
　　SCHUMANN: Aufträge / Aus den östlichen Rosen / Belsazar / Erstes Grün /
　　　　Freisinn / Hochländers Abschied / Jasminenstrauch / Meine Rose
　　WOLF: Drei Gedichte von Michelangelo / Harfenspieler Lieder
Harold Enns, bs-bar; Peggy Sheffield, pf.

PHILIPS

6520002. *Schubert and Schumann.*
SCHUBERT: An die Musik / An Sylvia / Auf dem Wasser zu singen / Die Forelle / Lachen und Weinen / Lied eines Schiffers an die Dioskuren / Der Wanderer / Der Wanderer an den Mond
SCHUMANN: Dichterliebe
Herman Prey, bar; Leonard Hokanson, pf.

6500282. *Elizabethan Lute Songs and Solos.*
CAMPION: It fell on a summer's day / Shall I come sweet love to thee? / Thy cypress curtain of the night
CUTTING: Galliard in Gm (lute)
DOWLAND: Awake sweet love thou art returned / Away with these self-loving lads / Come again, sweet love / Fine knack for ladies / Galliard in D (lute) / I saw my lady weep / In darkness let me dwell / Shall I sue / Tarletones Risurrectione (lute) / What if I never speed?
MORLEY: Come sorrow come / It was a lover and his lass / Thyrsis and Milla
ROSSETER: Sweet come again / What then is love but mourning / Whether men to laugh or weep
Frank Patterson, ten; Robert Spencer, lt.

6500412. *Lieder Recital.*
MAHLER: Ich bin der Welt abhanden gekommen / Das irdische Leben / Liebst du um Schönheit / Urlicht / Wo die schönen Trompeten blasen
SCHUBERT: Ellens Gesänge / Schwestergruss / Der Zwerg
Jessye Norman, sop; Irwin Gage, pf.

PLEIADES

P 103. *Italian Cantatas of the 17th and early 18th Centuries.*
CESTI: Languia già l'alba
ROSSI: Horche l'oscuro manto
SCARLATTI: Al fin m'ucciderete
STRADELLA: A quel candido foglio
Sylvia Stahlman, sop; Albert Fuller, hpsch.

RCA

CRM-3-0308. *Heldentenor of the Century.*
BRAHMS: Auf dem Kirckhofe
GRIEG: Eros / Ich liebe dich / En svane
JORDON: Hører Du / Drick
LA FORGE: Into the night
LEONCAVALLO: Vesti la guibba (Pagliacci) / No, Pagliacci non son
SIBELIUS: Svarta Rosor
SJÖBERG: Tonera
STRAUSS: Cäcilie / Heimliche Aufforderung / Traum durch die Dämmerung / Zueignung
TRUNK: Mir träumte von einen Königskind / Stille Lied
WAGNER: Götterdämmerung: Zu neuen Taten. Lohengrin: In fernem Land / Mein lieber Schwann. Die Meistersinger: Am stillen Herd / Prize Song. Parsifal: Anfortas, Sie Wunde / Nur eine Waffe taugt. Siegfried: Nothung, Nothung / Schmiede mein Hammer. Tannhäuser: Dir töne Lob / Rome Narrative. Tristan und Isolde: Love Duet / Die Walküre: Finale of Act I. Wesendonck Lieder: Schmerzen / Träume
WOLF: Schon streckt ich aus im Bett / Ein Ständchen Euch zu bringen
Lauritz Melchior, ten; Helen Traubel, sop; Kirsten Flagstad, sop; Ignace Strasfogel, pf; Philadelphia Orch: Ormandy; NBC Sym. Toscanini; San Francisco Sym. McArthur, Cleva.

RICHMOND

R 23184. *Lieder Recital.*
> **SCHUBERT:** An die Musik / Gretchen am Spinnrade / Die junge Nonne / Der Musensohn
> **SCHUMANN:** Frauenliebe und Leben / Volksliedchen / Widmung
> **WOLF:** Auf ein altes Bild / Auf einer Wanderung / Der Gärtner / Verborgenheit
> Kathleen Ferrier, con; John Newmark, pf; Phyllis Spurr, pf.

R 23187. *Broadcast Recital of English Songs.*
> **BRIDGE:** Go not happy day
> **HANDEL:** How changed the vision / Like as the love-lorn turtle
> **PARRY:** Love is a bable
> **PURCELL:** Hark! the echoing air / Mad Bess of Bedlam
> **STANFORD:** The Fairy Lough / A soft day
> **VAUGHAN WILLIAMS:** Silent noon
> **WARLOCK:** Pretty ring-time / Sleep
> Kathleen Ferrier, con; Phyllis Spurr, pf; Frederick Stone, pf.

ROCOCO

5350. *Songs by Richard Strauss and Erich Korngold.*
> **KORNGOLD:** Fern von Dir (Viel larm um Nichts) / Glück mir verblieb (Die tote Stadt)
> **STRAUSS:** All mein Gedanken / Breit über mein Haupt / Cäcilie / Du meines Herzens Krönelein / Freundliche Vision / Heimkehr / Heimliche Aufforderung / Ich liebe dich / Ich schwebe / Ich trage meine Minne / Kling / Meinem Kinde / Die Nacht / Schlagende Herzen / Seitdem dein Aug' / Ständchen / Traum durch die Dämmerung / Waldseligkeit / Zueignung
> Rosette Anday, con; Anton Dermota, ten; Lea Piltti, sop; Maria Reining, sop; Richard Strauss, pf; Erich Korngold, pf.

TELEFUNKEN

SLT-43116. *Bel Canto Arias.*
> **GALUPPI:** Se sapeste o giovinotti
> **GASPARINI:** Primavera che tutt'amorosa
> **HASSE:** Tradir sapeste, o perfidi
> **LEO:** Son qual nave in ria procella
> **MARCELLO:** Col pianto e coi sospiri / Latte e miele ecco vegg'io
> **MONTEVERDI:** Ecco pur ch'a voi ritorno
> **SCARLATTI:** Rugiadose, odorose
> **STEFFANI:** A facile vittoria / Piangerete, io ben io so
> **TELEMANN:** Non ho più core
> Peter Schreier, ten; Kammerorchester Berlin: Koch

TITLE / FIRST LINE INDEX